"In a time where there is so much talk about opportunities and challenges related to life and ministry in cities, the suburbs can become an almost forgotten afterthought. And yet, if the heart and mission of God are focused on every single square inch of his universe (and they are), then the suburbs remain an important, not to mention strategic, place for Christ's kingdom to be planted, germinate, grow, and bless the world. Ashley has done a wonderful job in this volume laying out kingdom opportunities and challenges in the suburban space. I have learned a lot from her ideas. I trust that you will too."

Scott Sauls, senior pastor of Christ Presbyterian Church in Nashville, author of *Jesus Outside the Lines, Befriend*, and *From Weakness to Strength*

"Hales takes on the near hopeless cause of waking up suburbanites like me to see God's larger story for our lives. *Finding Holy in the Suburbs* is both thoughtful and practical, and I admire her fierce writing, challenging me to seek out what's holy in my unremarkable suburban life."

Dave Goetz, author of *Death by Suburb*

"Ashley Hales stands in the bold tradition of the ancient prophets. In her book *Finding Holy in the Suburbs*, she exposes the tinseled temptations of the suburbs and calls us to Christ and his ways of generous self-sacrifice. The book's vivid storytelling, biblical reflections, unabashed truth telling, and practical applications make it a worthy read for anyone no matter where they live."

Jen Pollock Michel, author of *Teach Us to Want* and *Keeping Place*

"*Finding Holy in the Suburbs* is manna for those who believe suburban living is akin to living in a shallow, plastic wilderness devoid of beauty and inspiration. And it is manna for those of us who don't find ourselves in the suburbs but who, nevertheless, have an insatiable longing for meaning and for home. Hales is chock-full of wisdom, gifting us with a beautiful theology of place. Hales is a theologian of our time—heed her."

Marlena Graves, author of *A Beautiful Disaster: Finding Hope in the Midst of Brokenness*

"Scripture tells us that God uses the places we live to draw us to him. In *Finding Holy in the Suburbs*, Ashley Hales connects the dots for those living in the abundance of the developed world. Drawing on theology, sociology, and her own story, Hales shows how houses, streets, stores, and even playgrounds can reveal our hopes, goals, and deeper longings. Whether you live in the suburbs or are responsible for the discipleship of those who do, this book will challenge you to think holistically about the spaces we inhabit and how those spaces ultimately shape our souls."

Hannah Anderson, author of *Humble Roots: How Humility Grounds and Nourishes Your Soul*

"With poignant clarity and expansive grace, Ashley Hales assures us that God works powerfully in the suburbs. She lays out the pathway toward a holy and purposeful existence in our neighborhoods, one that is full of wonderful paradoxes: risk in safety, sacrifice in abundance, and shalom in busyness. *Finding Holy in the Suburbs* will encourage anyone who desires greater, eternal riches far beyond the American dream."

Dorcas Cheng-Tozun, *Christianity Today* contributor, author of *Start, Love, Repeat*

"As a suburban dweller myself, I confess I had never given much thought to how my location was shaping my faith. Thankfully, Ashley Hales's book *Finding Holy in the Suburbs* opened my eyes to both the pitfalls and the possibilities of following Jesus in suburbia. Through a combination of theological depth and simple, practical steps, Hales provides a much-needed path of spiritual formation. I am both humbled and delighted to say I will never look at my community the same again."

Sharon Hodde Miller, author of *Free of Me*

"Not just for suburbanites, this book is for anyone who wrestles against competition or control. *Finding Holy in the Suburbs* inverts our suburban sensibilities, nudging us away from self-preservation and toward the beautiful catastrophe of kingdom living. Masterfully weaving personal reflection, research, and robust theology, Ashley Hales takes our hand and walks us home."

Shannan Martin, author of *The Ministry of Ordinary Places* and *Falling Free*

"For all of us, the Christian life must be embodied and lived in a given place. Even for those of us (like me) who have never lived in the suburbs, Ashley Hales's examination of her own location and context help us explore how we are formed by our own concrete community and geography. Her honest struggles with the false promises of consumerism, busyness, worship of safety, and other idols of our day will resonate with many, including us city dwellers. This book isn't just about the suburbs; it is about a woman who finds herself in a place she would not have chosen and seeks to learn what the incarnation, life, death, and resurrection of Jesus bring to bear on her own home, neighborhood, time, money, parenting, friendships, and life in this moment in history. With warmth, humor, and wisdom, she helps her readers—in their own lives and context—to do the same."

Tish Harrison Warren, priest in the Anglican Church of North America, author of *Liturgy of the Ordinary: Sacred Practices in Everyday Life*

"I live on the encroaching edge of suburbia, but, like many readers, I prefer to read books about country life. I opened *Finding Holy in the Suburbs* assuming it would be a book I needed more than I wanted, but only a few pages in, it became a book I couldn't put down. Ashley Hales writes about life in the suburbs with gentle wisdom, intellectual depth, and refreshing honesty. She offers hope where so many have offered only criticism or cynicism. By weaving clear advice and transformative practices with engaging personal stories, Ashley Hales helps us to become reoriented toward our true spiritual home while sinking our roots more deeply into the ground beneath our feet. *Finding Holy in the Suburbs* is good news and practical encouragement for all of us, in every place."

Christie Purifoy, author of *Roots and Sky: A Journey Home in Four Seasons*

"Ashley is the rare sort of writer, imaginative yet concrete, prophetic yet gentle. She only cuts where she can bring healing. She brings just this sort of writing to *Finding Holy in the Suburbs*. And whether you're a suburban dweller, city slicker, or rural resident, this book has a powerful word to say about place and belonging."

Seth Haines, author of *Coming Clean: A Story of Faith*

Foreword by Emily P. Freeman

FINDING HOLY

in the SUBURBS

Living Faithfully in the Land of Too Much

ASHLEY HALES

IVP Books

An imprint of InterVarsity Press
Downers Grove, Illinois

InterVarsity Press
P.O. Box 1400, Downers Grove, IL 60515-1426
ivpress.com
email@ivpress.com

InterVarsity Press® is the book-publishing division of InterVarsity Christian Fellowship/USA®, a movement of students and faculty active on campus at hundreds of universities, colleges, and schools of nursing in the United States of America, and a member movement of the International Fellowship of Evangelical Students. For information about local and regional activities, visit intervarsity.org.

Scripture quotations, unless otherwise noted, are from The Holy Bible, English Standard Version, copyright © 2001 by Crossway Bibles, a division of Good News Publishers. Used by permission. All rights reserved.

While any stories in this book are true, some names and identifying information may have been changed to protect the privacy of individuals.

Cover design and illustration: Autumn Short
Interior design: Daniel van Loon

ISBN 978-0-8308-4545-3 (print)
ISBN 978-0-8308-7397-5 (digital)

Printed in the United States of America ♾

InterVarsity Press is committed to ecological stewardship and to the conservation of natural resources in all our operations. This book was printed using sustainably sourced paper.

Library of Congress Cataloging-in-Publication Data
Names: Hales, Ashley, 1980- author.
Title: Finding holy in the suburbs : living faithfully in the land of too much / Ashley Hales ; foreword by Emily P. Freeman.
Description: Downers Grove : InterVarsity Press, 2018. | Includes bibliographical references.
Identifiers: LCCN 2018022673 (print) | LCCN 2018032049 (ebook) | ISBN 9780830873975 (eBook) | ISBN 9780830845453 (pbk. : alk. paper)
Subjects: LCSH: Christian life—United States. | Suburbanites—United States—Religious life.
Classification: LCC BR526 (ebook) | LCC BR526 .H245 2018 (print) | DDC 277.3/0091733—dc23
LC record available at https://lccn.loc.gov/2018022673

P   25   24   23   22   21   20   19   18   17   16   15   14   13   12   11   10   9   8   7   6   5   4   3

Y   38   37   36   35   34   33   32   31   30   29   28   27   26   25   24   23   22   21   20

To my husband,

BRYCE,

who, in helping me find holy in the suburbs,

has given me more of himself and more of God

CONTENTS

FOREWORD

Emily P. Freeman

IF THE SHUTTERS ARE OPEN in my bedroom and I look out across our cul-de-sac, I can see my brother-in-law's front porch without even lifting my head off my pillow. If I sit up a bit straighter and lean slightly forward, I can see my mother-in-law's entire house where it sits atop a small hill right next door to his. In the summer, the view is blocked partially by the leafy branches in our front yard, but in the winter we have a clear view of them and they have a clear view of us.

Out of the seven houses in our North Carolina cul-de-sac, three of them are filled with Freemans, is what I'm saying. Yes, I share a street with most of my in-laws. Whether you think that's lovely or weird, I agree—depending on the day.

We've lived a lot of regular life under these tree-lined streets, crossed these yards hundreds of times, watched cousins play, argue, make up, and play some more. In the elementary school years, we walked our kids together to school, joining up with some other neighbors who don't share our last name, a colorful posse of friends, acquaintances, and family armed with backpacks, lunch bags, and sometimes a stroller or dog, depending on the weather. All of our kids have learned to ride a bike around this circle, and in about a year my girls will learn to drive a car here too.

Sometimes when I think about my own setting, I wonder if it's okay. Are we embodying the gospel enough? Are we insulating ourselves from the world by living with people who not only share our lifestyle but also our last name? Can we image God from this regular, sensationless place where we live?

You have your own neighborhood, city street, or daily setting. Your place has characters, whether they are schoolmates or in-laws, friends or strangers. This book you're holding is about those everyday kinds of spaces. Because whether you live in a cul-de-sac, in a high-rise apartment, on a college campus, or on several acres of farmland, the truth is this book is not about where you live.

It's more about how you live there.

We all live in a cul-de-sac of sorts, though it may not always be shaped like a circle. We all have spaces we fold ourselves around and allow to shape us, for better or worse. Ashley Hales is a woman who knows that we are always being spiritually formed, but the question is by what and for what purpose? Are we bending our lives around the spaces we occupy, the things we acquire, the homes we build, and the positions we're climbing toward? Or are we willing to let the triune God straighten out the narrative of safety and control, and pull us closer into his story of love and belonging, one that turns out looking way different than we always thought?

Finding the sacred in the midst of everyday things is not a new conversation. But the best books aren't the ones that have all brand new information. We don't have context for that. Instead, we need new voices telling us old things, retelling us the Story we believe but forget, reminding us of who we are and where we belong. We need voices that are willing to enter into those conversations we are already having, taking place in our churches, our classrooms, our sidewalks, and inside our own heads. We need strong voices willing to walk along the regular streets with us in our everyday corners of the kingdom of God.

Ashley Hales is one of these kind and insightful new voices.

For those of us who grew up in the "do big things for God" youth group culture, we step into this conversation as adults with some hesitancy, some skepticism, and the smallest bit of hope. Could it be possible that starting small and staying put is not only okay but could actually be a worthy and holy calling? Ashley Hales says yes.

Come and walk beside her through the streets of her California suburb. Discover how these mundane places have shaped her life and notice all the ways it will mirror and inform your own.

INTRODUCTION

A Story to Find Home in the Geography of Nowhere

We can't locate ourselves, much less find
ourselves, apart from the places we inhabit.

LEONARD HJALMARSON, *NO HOME LIKE PLACE*

ON THE DAY THE MOVING TRUCK PULLED AWAY, I was the last to leave. The walls were empty except for the black and white stripes we'd painted, and that little spot of white on the turquoise kitchen wall we covered up with a frame (thinking one day we'd get around to fixing it). There was no bump-bump of children running up and down stairs, no circles of noisemaking.

I stepped on the floorboard that always creaks—to hear it one last time. What was once something to fix was now dear.

I ran my fingers along the living room walls. "Thank you," I said as I touched the walls that had seen so much life, tantrums, tears, and laughter. "Thank you, thank you, thank you."

I walked around the room, blessing this house, caressing it like the lips of a lover and bade it to hold our love well. I prayed the house would be a sieve where our crazy would get caught and our love would pour out to the next owners, another pastor's family.

This move from an urban neighborhood in Salt Lake City back home to the suburbs of Southern California was clearly where God was calling us next, but that did not mean the leave-taking did not also feel like death. This was the longest home we'd ever known as husband and wife. We brought home half our children to this spot of earth. This was the house with the fifteen-year renovation dreams attached to it. This was the house with the bookshelves my husband, Bryce, built for me to hold the weight of my years of study.

We were leaving the creaking hundred-year-old floorboards Bryce had refinished to follow God's call to plant a church in the land of plenty and cookie-cutter tract homes. Roots, when exposed to the light, quiver a little.

At first, I scoffed at the idea of a suburban church plant. I thought I was too good for the suburbs, too good to move back home. If you gave me a life in the city or the country I could idealize it to death, cover it in metaphors, and figure out what the kingdom of God looked like with art galleries and public transportation or endless space for my children to run.

This move, however, pulled me up short. My self-narrative for the past two decades had revolved around movement and moving place. As a married couple, we've moved eight times, birthed more children than we planned, and now find ourselves not living a life overseas or in the heart of a bustling cultural center. Instead, we were moving home—to the suburbs. We would be two miles from the hospital where my husband was born.

Some people crave the rootedness and security of staying put. I have measured my distance from home as markers of belonging. Each one—Los Angeles, Edinburgh, Los Angeles (again), San Diego, Salt Lake City—as evidence that we were doing significant things for God. From there it was a quick jump to seeing our worth lay in our geography.

For a woman who craved the cultural hub of a city or the idyllic freedom of a rural life, I bristled about a move to the suburbs. I was happy in Salt Lake City. The city was booming: ski resorts were a short drive away, diversity was increasing as more immigrants moved in, and restaurants were popping up with award-winning international cuisines downtown.

Moving home held out its charms: I was excited about proximity to family, how a newer house meant less things falling apart than in our old house, and we wouldn't have to learn a new place. But, I wondered, how would I find belonging in the suburbs where everyone—even their houses—looked the same?

I craved sustainability, depth, meaning, nuance—the things you find in a city, I reasoned, or at least in the type of rural life championed by Wendell Berry. How did this move fit; how could *I* fit? Underneath this superiority was a deep fear that I couldn't cut it: I wasn't pretty enough or successful enough. Could I find belonging in the suburbs, or would I be a misfit?

I'm comforted by the biblical precedent of God's people laughing at his plans—backing into corners and running off in the opposite direction. I feel kin to Jonah, thinking he was too good for a place; to Sarah, laughing that God could do the impossible; to Moses, thinking he didn't have the right skill set to serve God's people; to Joshua, who was afraid; to David, who followed his feelings, which lead to adultery and murder; to Peter, who said he'd always come through and then ran away; to Paul, who desperately wanted to do everything right. The list goes on. In each story, God restores.

So I took a deep breath, said goodbye, and closed the door to our life in Salt Lake City. This was it—we were moving to the suburbs.

THE GEOGRAPHY OF NOWHERE

I realized as the moving truck pulled away from our Salt Lake City home, I couldn't use my place to make me feel special and unique. I'd turned my nose up at the suburbs, thinking they were only superficial and image obsessed, and their residents were unconcerned with real problems. But I knew there was more, and I knew I was called to love not only individual people but also my place. Moving home to the suburbs, I longed to discern how to faithfully live in the land of too much.

I used to think nothing of my suburban childhood, how each "city" bled into the other, without distinctiveness. I enjoyed the chain stores and was used to driving everywhere. Only when I grew older and moved away did I see how each place formed my loves. Each place fashions what we value. Places form our loves.

Are the suburbs really the "geography of nowhere" that Harold Kunstler calls them? Could a land of commuters, tract homes, strip malls, and ease actually malform our souls? And if we're Christians, how might we live

Places form our loves.

a full Christian life in the suburbs—do we even notice how the suburbs shape our souls? Should we feel guilty for our privilege, or should we just move?

More than 50 percent of Americans live in suburbs, and many of them desire to live a Christian life. Yet often the suburbs are ignored ("Your place doesn't matter, we're all going to heaven anyway"), denigrated and demeaned ("You're selfish if you live in a suburb; you only care about your own safety and advancement"), or seen as a cop-out to a faithful Christian life ("If you really loved God, you'd move to Africa or work in an impoverished area"). From books to Hollywood jokes, the suburbs aren't supposed to be good for our souls.

Even David Goetz's popular book, *Death by Suburb*, though helpful, presumes suburban life is toxic for your soul—as if suburbia were uniquely broken by the weight of sin. The suburbs—like any place— exhibit both the goodness of God's creative acts (in desiring to foster community, beauty, rest, hospitality, family) and sin (in focusing on image, materialism, and individualism to the exclusion of others). We cannot be quick to dismiss the suburbs out of hand.

STORIES OF THE SUBURB

In what they center and in what they hide, all places tell stories through their geography, architecture, and city planning. After World War II, suburbs popped up across America. They were places upwardly mobile middle-class residents would retreat to in their version of a country manor house placed at a reasonable distance away from the city, where (usually) men worked.

Houses became status markers. Cars and commuting became more prevalent. Women increasingly stayed home, removed from the bustle of city life. As suburbs grew, they became whiter and richer: their racial, ethnic, and socioeconomic diversity wasn't just lowered, the suburbs "built inequality to last."

Today, each suburb is different: some are receiving previous urban dwellers who can't afford city life

> **Thankfully, the good news of the gospel is never defined by a ZIP code.**

when they have a family; others are the result of "white flight"; still others are more affluent and cost-prohibitive than the cities they orbit. Many are growing in their racial, political, and socioeconomic diversity.

But each suburb in its own way evangelizes for the good life: a life of safety, beauty, comfort, and ease. Suburbs, like all places, reflect both our good, God-given desires to create home, and also the brokenness of a place in their geography, entry systems, and laws. Thankfully, the good news of the gospel is never defined by a ZIP code.

The gospel story both helps us see the idols of our suburbs and brings hope for an abundant life not contingent on our circumstances.

We make our home by stories, it's said that author Flannery O'Connor wrote. In my move to the suburbs, I knew I needed a new story to bring me back home. Daily, I need a new narrative to help me find both the holy in the suburbs and a story bigger and better than my cul-de-sac.

Jesus tells a parable about a father and his lost boy; I turn to this parable of the prodigal son when the suburbs tell me I'm not enough.

A STORY TO FIND HOME

There once was a man with two sons. He had the good life in the palm of his hand, with his flocks, herds, and land that stretched as far as the horizon. His sons were hearty and good, and he dreamed of how they'd inherit the land.

But one day, his younger son broke his heart. It was not surprising; he'd always been a free spirit, motivated by pleasure. That's what made the man's eyes sparkle, seeing his beloved son drinking down the dregs of the blessings of the land they shared. The younger son boldly asked for his share of the property. He didn't want the father. He wanted the father's stuff.

Surprisingly, the father gave it. There was no quick way to liquidate an estate. He sold off land and herds, and looked the fool to the neighboring village. They must've talked about how he'd lost his marbles. How could he dote on such a drunkard son who didn't even love, let alone respect, all the hard work his father had done? How could he be so lavish? At least he had the eldest, responsible son, they said.

So the younger son, with his sack of coins and his donkey, went off to a faraway land. This place, unlike his father's, would satisfy him. His kingdom stretched to the horizon, and he picked out pleasure like grapes. He touched each one and watched them all go down. The wine was smooth.

Meanwhile, back at home, the old man sat on the porch, often standing up scanning the horizon. The path was always empty. His boy was not coming home.

Finally the young man's money ran out. He couldn't go home. What option did he have? He went to all his friends who had gathered around his table, but they didn't want him now, not without the wine. The only job was feeding a rich man's pigs.

Living day by day in the pigs' slop—with the filth collecting around his ankles—was dark, but also strangely comforting. He could do his grieving in private. He raised his fist to the heavens at the unfairness of it all. Finally, after the shouting, he became unfeeling, quiet, slopping pails of food to troughs and numbing himself in the monotony of work. In the dark nights, he'd dream of home, of simple and abundant food.

His body ached with a hunger that was bottomless.

Yet, as the dreams took over his waking hours, he too awoke. He remembered himself. Maybe his father would take him back. He could be his father's hired servant. At least then he'd get out of the pig slop. So he got up and began the long walk home.

The miles were long and he rehearsed his speech, "Father, I've sinned against heaven and before you. I am no longer worthy to be called your son. Treat me as one of your hired servants." He didn't deserve even that, but maybe his father would be compassionate, maybe he could work his way back home.

Midweek the old man sat anxiously scanning the horizon, as he did every day. His land was smaller now, but that wasn't what he was inspecting. His eyes hungered for his boy.

But today, today! There was a speck! He picked up his robes and ran like a little boy. He ran faster and faster, motivated by an overwhelming love that gave breath to his tired lungs. His boy had come home!

When he got to his younger son, he covered him in kisses, like he'd done when the boy was fresh from the womb. The son didn't know what to do—he'd vowed to work, so he started his speech, but his father shouted to his servants, "Bring quickly the best robe, and put it on him, and put a ring on his hand, and shoes on his feet. And bring the fattened calf and kill it, and let us eat and celebrate. For this my son was dead, and is alive again; he was lost, and is found."

The feast was lavish and the wine didn't stop. The whole village turned up to see the miracle—to see the boy who had been brought back to life, the boy who had gone away and was hard on his father, who now wasn't turned away but welcomed like a king.

Meanwhile the older son was in the field, and as he came near the house he heard music and dancing. A servant told him his brother had come back and the party was for him. The older brother ran off to the edge of the field, threw his shoes off in a rage. Bitterness and envy snaked around his heart.

But his father saw his older son too and left the feast to find his boy. The father gently asked why the eldest wouldn't join the feast; he entreated his son to come in. It seemed obvious to the older son. He railed, "Look, these many years I have served you, and I never disobeyed your command, yet you never gave me a young goat that I might celebrate with my friends. But when this son of yours came, who has devoured your property buying prostitutes, you killed the fattened calf for him!" He spun and twisted; his words were like venom. Shouldn't his own behavior be the praise of the village and the centerpiece of the feast? How could love be so wild and extravagant?

It was all *his*, in fact. When his father had divided up the property to give to the younger brother, all that the father had left rightfully belonged to the older son. This son was stuck between desperately wanting to let go of control, of rightness, to join the party, and on the other hand wondering if he did so, if giving up all his work, all the responsibility, all his rights, would render him invisible. Powerless. Equal with his brother.

The father continued, "Son, you are always with me, and all that is mine is yours. It was fitting to celebrate and be glad, for this your brother was dead, and is alive; he was lost, and is found." The son felt an inward prick. The words stung. But was there healing to be found on the other edge of pain? And how indeed could love be so lavish?

Is there really a welcome home for all of us?

This story of the prodigal son can feel a bit tired and worn if you've been around church much. Yet we need to rehear it because the suburbs are full of younger brothers trying to clean up their act to be accepted—to work harder, be responsible, and tone down impulse and pleasure to fit in to a buttoned-up world.

The suburbs are also full of elder brothers turning their nose up at the lavishness of grace, because, after all, the story goes, we've worked hard for what we've earned. Yet this is just one place in Scripture where God shows us who he is: a loving father and a gracious host.

This story shows us our deep hunger to belong, to find home, to root ourselves in place, and how, when we're hungry, we fill ourselves up with other things that promise to sate our hungers instead of running home to our Father.

Our places are good gifts; home is how we begin to know who we are. Yet when we use the gifts of our places—when we use the suburbs—as "ultimate things," like pastor Tim Keller is fond of saying, we worship them.

This book is a gentle call to all of us in the suburbs to come home, to find belonging not in what we buy or how we constantly center ourselves, but in loving God and our neighbor.

If God is our host who prepares a table for us and the bread of life we feast on, then he is intimately concerned with our hungers. He's concerned about meeting our physical and existential rumblings.

HUNGRY IN THE SUBURBS

Suburbs seek to fill good hungers by offering us the suburban gods of consumerism, individualism, busyness, and safety. When we glut ourselves on the food of the suburbs, we are left with aching bellies. But graciously, God always meets our hungers with himself. Being hungry in the suburbs is a sign to point us home. Healing begins at the place of hunger.

The thing about hungers is that they are all best met in God alone.

Breathe easy—the story of God's kingdom is not about morality and upright living. It's not about a bigger house, more

> Healing begins at the place of hunger.

resources (even to give away), security, safety, or the next promotion. No, the story of the Bible is that we have a Father God who meets us in our lostness, in whatever form that takes: lost in our gluttony and lust, or in our upright behavior.

The story of the Bible is that there is no place or people too small for God to come and get you. We choose to forfeit the wildness of belonging to God when we settle for creating our own way in the suburbs.

Our souls suffer in the suburbs when we have the financial means to always fill our needs, where we sleep on featherbeds and eat rich food. If famines and failure do not lead us to see our bloated but starving souls, then, as people on the Way, we must practice the discipline of being curious about our small hunger pains. This hurts. It brings us to our knees when we realize our hungers have been numbed.

But until we take away all the fast-food fixes we don't realize our hunger is still there, and more than that, that there is a gift wrapped up in the unraveling. Not until we feel our hunger can we be propelled toward repentance, vulnerability, welcome, and belonging where we're held securely in a grip that is not our own.

Feeling our hunger is the first step toward remembering who we are.

We need a story to find home in the suburbs. Indeed, as Albert Hsu writes in *The Suburban Christian*, "God needs suburban Christians who are willing to take a sharp look at their environment, recognize the challenges of the suburban setting, and then *stay here* to do something about it." This book is that story.

THE ROAD AHEAD

The impulse for building the suburbs was to create an idyll: the best of the country with access to the city, the leisure of a country manor, a place of safety, and strong, thriving communities. These are good hungers: to enjoy, to rest, to work well, to keep your family safe, and to grow a cohesive community. But when these hungers are met simply through shiny suburban packages, they come out sideways as consumerism, individualism, busyness, and exclusion. There is a better way for the suburbs.

This book is about coming home, about finding ourselves in the story of God and rooting ourselves in our places. It's a bold look at the culture of affluence as expressed in suburban life. My hope is that it challenges your idea of belonging and also shows you a more beautiful story to root yourself in. As individuals, families, and churches commit to love and sacrifice for our neighborhoods and subdivisions, we will find our place.

God has made us hungry people, and our hungers are best met with him. In each chapter, I will name a particular human hunger (such as having good work to do, to be significant or safe), and then examine how the suburbs seek to fill that hunger (in a less wholesome, fast-food version). Finally I lay out a few small habits to reorient our hungers Godward.

The first third of the book examines idols particular to the suburbs: consumerism, individualism, busyness, and safety. Our fingers are pried off our idols when we repent. The middle of the book focuses on repentance and living out of a deep storehouse of belovedness. This is the antidote to suburban idols. The final third of the book takes up particular practices, or counterliturgies—these are different stories we enact in the suburbs so our hungers are met with God rather than the idols of our place. These are hospitality, generosity, vulnerability, and shalom (seeking the wholeness of the suburbs).

To help you as you read, each chapter ends with several practical counterliturgies (or new habits of seeing, being, and doing) or positive practices to help you begin to live out the gospel in your subdivision.

Finding Holy in the Suburbs is best read in community. Your neighborhood's needs are different than mine. Suburbs come in all shapes and sizes. You'll need people on the ground with you to commit to staying put and starting small. As you meet around tables, you and your neighbors can share stories of conviction, hope, and transformation. At the end of the book, you'll find discussion questions to help guide your time together.

Are you ready to begin? To find an adventure that's not contingent on your bank account, who you know, or even on your circumstances? Come and join me—it's time to find holy in the suburbs.

1

Worshiping Granite Countertops

CONSUMERISM

*Because our consumption can take us
anywhere, we are nowhere in particular.*

WILLIAM T. CAVANAUGH, *BEING CONSUMED*

SHORTLY AFTER WE MOVED, I walked into my new suburban Target and felt like I was stuck in a maze. This reiteration of my favorite place to drool over trendy home decor, clothes, and office supplies was the flip-flop layout from my Salt Lake City Target. It was the same place, but it was completely different. For weeks, I kept pushing my cart toward the automotive supplies in the back corner when I thought I was headed to the checkout line. Eventually, I learned a new way through this familiar but not-quite-the-same space, and my new layout became the default. In the turmoil of moving, Target was still a welcome point of reference.

Target offered rest. It provided a feeling of home: I could imagine myself back in Salt Lake City with a mountainscape outside rather than more big-box buildings. Beyond that, temporally, there was a texture of all the accumulated years of red shopping carts, children running to climb the balls outside of the store, and the allure of dollar bins. In Target, I could belong to a tribe of tired mothers searching for relief.

I'd wandered Target's aisles for years with strollers, and single carts, and even the ones that fit three kids with my fourth strapped on me.

(Those years are blurry.) I'd pushed my oldest child as a toddler in a fold-up umbrella stroller in the suburbs of San Diego when we needed free air conditioning and something to do. I'd had impromptu dance parties with my kids in the aisles of my Salt Lake City Target. After tantrums that had gotten out of hand, I'd even abandoned carts in Target, a child under each arm like footballs, while my older children stomped and glared because we were leaving. (That was fun. I ignored the staring customers.)

Target shopping trips had become an unthinking liturgy—what I did to bide the time or to reward myself for the hard work of parenting, while also feeling rather self-righteous since I could productively get errands done too. I could buy whatever struck my fancy (or at least imagine doing so) while sipping my Starbucks latte.

Each time I ventured into Target, I could be assured of air conditioning, my favorite clothes on sale, and overhead lighting that didn't make me want to run for the hills.

I could imagine myself in their home displays, how the art supplies would make me a crafty mom, how if I bought that dish soap we'd finally keep our kitchen clean and tidy, how I'd drink more water when I had the new glass water bottle, how I'd finally find the right concealer to make me look awake and fresh, and how the right hair product would give me beachy waves. I'd dream about how I could totally rock fringe booties and gladiator sandals, especially when they were on clearance.

A shopping trip to Target held out the adrenaline rush of a good deal, the mingling of caffeine with the dopamine hit when we buy something, the pleasure of comfort, and the hope of transformation (at least regarding new footwear). If my children decided my Target deal-finding mission was not their jam for the day, I could (usually) bribe them with snacks, goodies from the dollar bin, or an impromptu lunch at the adjoining Pizza Hut. At Target I could morph into "fun mom": "Sure you can have Goldfish or Pokémon cards! And sure, let's grab new swim goggles and new markers, as long as Mama can look at the boho chic rugs, gold office supplies, and comb through the sale racks!"

I was multitasking and being productive—doing the errands, taking a break, buying a coffee, indulging my children a little. We all need a little retail therapy, right? Right?

GOLDEN CALVES

Those of us who are people of faith tend to worship our place alongside God. Sure, we love Jesus, but in the suburbs we'd like our slice of the American dream too. We want our Bible studies alongside our Target splurges. It's not wrong to appreciate beauty, to buy things, or want our homes to be lovely. Shopping itself isn't bad, but our repeated habits help to form our loves. When I buy dark chocolate or new throw pillows when I'm feeling lonely, sad, or angry, I only mask my soul hunger with a suburban fast-food fix. Since the Garden of Eden, and just like the prodigal son, we leave home to seek it elsewhere—even in new home decor or packed schedules. When I go to Target to solve my locational and existential homesickness, it will never work. Because Target can never sate my hungers. *what does this have to do w/ suburbs?*

We keep shopping, buying, and consuming because we are desperate to be filled without it seeming like joy and happiness always find a way to leak out. We crave belonging and rootedness. We want a home. God designed us for himself; we are restless until we rest in God, as Augustine said.

But the more I use stuff to fill up my hungers, the more distance I put between God and myself. And as I continue to fill up my infinite hungers with finite things (when I run through the Starbucks drive-through as an answer to my weariness or feeling out of place), these finite things not only leave me hungry but also create ways of being— or liturgies—that move me away from God.

Soon I'm unthinkingly buying note cards in the dollar bins at Target every time I feel lonely. I buy chocolate when I'm depressed or needy.

I buy facial masks because I fear the unknown of aging. I buy notebooks to keep our family organized, but more than that, to maintain a semblance of control.

Our eyes drift to the new, the flashy, the trendy, just like Eve's eyes lit up before she took the fruit God told her not to eat; just like the younger son was tantalized by the far-off country. We leave the goodness of God and our first home, and set up our tents elsewhere, just like God's people.

After God's people had been exiled from the Garden, they grew in number and influence, yet were finally taken as slaves in Egypt. After hundreds of years of slavery, God delivered his people through miracles. As they wander the desert as a consequence for their disobedience, God gives them instructions about how to set up the tabernacle, a movable space to worship God living among them.

Between instructions for the tabernacle's construction and its execution, Moses is at the top of Mount Sinai receiving God's law for forty days. Aaron, his brother, is in the camp below with the people. They get impatient. They grumble. They gather around Aaron, tell him to get up and ask him to "make us gods who shall go before us" (Exodus 32:1). In their disdain, their leader becomes "*this* Moses," "*the man* who brought us out from Egypt," and Aaron (perhaps sheepishly, or as their puppet, or just unsure what to do) instructs the people to take off their gold earrings. He then fashions their gold into a calf. They proclaim, "These are your gods, O Israel, who brought you up out to the land of Egypt!" (Exodus 32:4). And Aaron, perhaps as a way to stay true to God, sets up an altar next to the calf, and proclaims the next day a feast to the Lord.

God's people exchange the glory of the living and true God with the earrings that were in their ears mere hours before. Israel attributes their salvation to the gold in their ears. The statue of a calf seems primitive, but we are no different.

Salvation, in its general sense, connotes "preservation from destruction, ruin, loss or calamity." Tell me if you do not use your house, your 401(k), your savings account, your job, and your marriage as bulwarks to push off ruin, loss, and calamity. It is not that institutions or buildings are bad things. These stabilizing features of our lives, though, easily morph into salvific things. They also shine and shimmer in the ear. They are not the things that deliver us.

But when objects and relationships move from lovely things into salvific things, we do exactly the same as God's people lost in the wilderness. Ask yourself, *Where do I run when I experience negative emotions*—is it food, a listening ear, shopping, drinks, exercise? Or do we first bring our fear, angst, and impatience to a God who can actually do something about it? When we get antsy waiting on God and his word, we ask our stuff to save us.

We want God *and* the stuff we worship alongside God.

We may still do all the right things in the suburbs: we show up to church. We give money away. We like the gods of our own hands right next to the altar of the Lord. Yet worship is never simply what we do

> When we get antsy waiting on God and his word, we ask our stuff to save us.

with our Sunday mornings: it is a posture, an attitude, and a heart orientation toward that which holds our affections.

When Aaron set up the altar next to the calf, he thought the people could have it all. They could use a golden calf to make ritual offerings and perform sexual rites just like other nations. But as John L. Mackay notes in his commentary on this passage, "God's people are not freed so that they may go their own way. They are saved so that they may realise the purposes of God." We are saved for God, not for ourselves. Freedom is not freedom *from* all constraints on an individual: freedom is abundant life *in* Christ *for* others.

We worship what saves us. We may not worship gold earrings, but we feel better about ourselves when we invite others over to admire our new kitchen renovation or bathroom remodel or our photos from our cruise. This God-as-gold comes in smaller suburban packages too: we share our Target haul, our thrift-store deals, and how buying a cute set of yellow throw pillows on sale at HomeGoods literally turned our day around (ask me how I know). We're impatient. We seek the hit of retail therapy to replace the deep, abiding sense of belonging with the God of the universe. Consumerism isn't just buying material things we need, rather, "consumerism is a type of spirituality." That is why Moses reacts so strongly.

This is why it feels so appropriate—like the end of a Greek play where all is set right—that after Moses sees what's happened he not only breaks the tablets of God's law in anger but also burns the golden calf, turns it into powder, and makes the people drink it. It's as if Moses says, in making their golden calf green juice, "Let me show you what your gods are made of: they are but dust, particles that pass through your stomach and are turned into excrement. They can never feed and nourish you. They move through your gut and do not embolden or empower you. They do not slake your thirst. They do not meet your hunger. All that gods of gold are good for is to be turned into waste."

When we try to feed ourselves with the shiny packaging of our things, we go hungry every time. We're left malnourished and empty and longing for the next thing to scratch an internal itch.

LITURGIES OF CONSUMERISM

Retail therapy gives us the thrill of the hunt and a hit of dopamine (the love hormone) as we anticipate a purchase, but it cannot feed our hungers. We know this. But we return each time, hoping it will. We buy and we window shop because we aren't captivated by a better way, a better story. The process of finding holy in the suburbs is not necessarily eschewing Target runs, but it starts by waking up to our hungers in the first place.

Our hunger is human: we want to be filled. We desire abundance and satiety. We want to belong to a people and a place.

In the suburbs we settle for consumerism to answer our hunger to be whole. "There is an intimate and indissoluble link between suburbia and buying," writes Roger Silverstone. Buying has become our favorite form of worship.

We stuff ourselves with stuff, thinking more, bigger, and better will make us feel less empty or alone.

In his book *Desiring the Kingdom*, James K. A. Smith writes of

> Buying has become our favorite form of worship.

the mall as a religious space. In this religious space, we are motivated by our felt needs: "we come looking, not sure what for, but expectant, knowing that what we need must be here." In this worshipful space of the mall, we take off our earrings and hope they turn into gods who save—whether that's to stave off boredom, or to feel as if we are creating a home or a body that is beautiful and inviting, or to get a rush from whatever is new, novel, and numbs our ache when all is not right with the world. We ask what we buy to save us.

When we have our "newfound holy object in hand, we proceed to the altar, which is the consummation of worship. . . . This is a religion of transaction, of exchange and communion. . . . And so we make our sacrifice, leave our donation, but in return receive something with solidity that is wrapped in the colors and symbols of the saints and the season." Buying is our suburban form of worship, whether it's at the mall or shopping from our phones.

As the Israelites grew impatient for God, they filled up their time with worship, but it was something shiny and new, something they could see and touch. The golden god wasn't intended as a replacement for God, it was a bookmark for him until he came back. But when we bookmark things in God's place—from our children to our spouses, from our God-given work to our volunteering or our stuff—these good gifts from God are transformed into shiny objects we worship.

They become dust destined for the toilet; we're just too enamored by the sheen to realize it.

When our lives are based on the story of the marketplace, we do not move toward others (God or neighbor). Because we're fighting to acquire (stuff, reputation, you name it), we lose out on living from a deep storehouse of belovedness. Our relationships are ruled by liturgies of transaction. When he gives, I repay. When a relationship becomes boring like last year's styles, we throw out the old and begin anew (or at least move that relationship to the back of the closet). We value people for what they do for us rather than as fellow human beings created to enjoy God and made in his image.

Then, God's church is less family—where a person is joyful, vulnerable, annoyed, and hurt, but deeply committed to working things out—and more about which brand appeals to my sensibilities the most. If we treat God's church like check boxes of our personal preferences, how can we expect our deep hungers to be met? The church is not a check box. It is God's people on mission together. What is more exciting and fulfilling than that?

We are formed by our daily habits. What, how, when, from where, and how much we purchase aren't just morally neutral consumer choices defined by the best deal. They actually shape our hearts. They tell us who and what we worship. When I wake in the morning, pour myself a cup of fancy coffee on my granite countertop, shove prepackaged food into lunch boxes, and pour the latest cereal out for my children, I'm formed by what and how I buy. What I value is often ease over justice: I have no connection to my food or coffee. I neglect to discover the working conditions of the coffee bean workers if I don't buy fair-trade. I value quantity over quality all in an effort to save time or money. I functionally center myself over the stories and even livelihoods of others by how I buy and how I spend my time.

Yet, at the same time, I realize many people aren't able to make the same choices with their money. They survive, and coffee (let alone granite countertops) is a luxury. But if you or I have been given forms of economic or locational privilege, do we use it to make our lives more comfortable, or do we use our privilege for others?

Along with Tish Harrison Warren, we must ask the hard question, What if "my daily practices [are] malforming me, making me less alive, less human, less able to give and receive love throughout my day"? What if, like golden earrings and golden calves, I'm expecting my granite countertops to save me?

The granite countertops of course are not the thing, and it's easy to replace our desire for nice things with more "acceptable" forms of affection: love, service, justice, and love for our children. The question is, what is underneath the surface? If I decide to be morally upright and change my thinking about my pretty kitchen but do not interrogate the habits of my heart, I am no better off. It is both about countertops and not about countertops at all. Am I concerned about fitting into a story of affluence? Do I feel entitled to a certain level of privilege and comfort? What has captured my imagination: my countertops or the kingdom of God?

— where is the line?

By elevating the thing itself to godlike heights, we lose the goodness of the original. When we require a prince to rescue us, we spoil the goodness of actual husbands. When we serve our jobs, our children's wishes, or our new granite countertops, the things are destined to turn to dust in our hands. Though it smarts and feels like death, the crumbling is a gift.

Carol Ann Duffy writes her poem "Mrs. Midas" from the perspective of the woman married to King Midas (the man who wished for everything he touched to be turned to gold). After he comes home with his wish granted, Mrs. Midas makes him sleep in the spare bedroom, afraid for her life, yet reflects on their separation:

You see, we were passionate then,
in those halcyon days: unwrapping each other, rapidly,
like presents, fast food. But now I feared his honeyed
    embrace,
the kiss that would turn my lips to a work of art.

Our desires easily ruin the thing itself when the object of our desires moves from its proper place. After King Midas has moved out, delirious with gold and hearing the song of Pan in the woods, his wife, alone, stops dead in her tracks seeing a bowl of apples. The poem ends: "I miss most / even now, his hands, his warm hands on my skin, his touch." When apples have turned to gold, they lose what they're meant for. When people are golden objects, we lose connection. Likewise, when we require our people and our things to stand in God's place, we lose the goodness of the original.

Our liturgies of consumerism do more than ruin God's blessings. They are poor substitutes for belonging. When we buy, we're buying the dreams associated with the nouns we say we want. We buy the feeling and the promise. As Neil Cummings and Marysia Lewandowska note, "It is not objects that people really desire, but their lush coating of images and dreams. . . . It is never the object which is consumed—instead it is the relationship between us and the object of desire." Flat abs will never satisfy. Neither will the luxury vehicle, more square footage, perfectly behaved children, or that new pair of shoes. Your children's academic accolades and athletic prowess will never be enough. They all demand more to keep the dream alive. Your vacations or investments or marital bliss will fail and falter.

When we keep purchasing, keep consuming, and keep envying and coveting, we are pining for what the objects represent: peace, ease, meaning, beauty, stability, adventure, knowledge, renown, connection, and esteem. Such heavyweight abstract ideas cannot be saddled to the latest purchase. Granite countertops are a poor substitute for peace, beauty, and belonging.

Like God's people, we lose sight of what's really going on under the surface. If we are wrapped up in God's story, we already have belonging. But—perhaps especially in suburbia—we continue to buy our dreams because we have the resources and privilege to do so. We equate security with a number in the bank or on the scale. We think freedom is found in what we drive or where we live. Rest is how, where, and when we vacation. Peace is defined by the absence of responsibility. All our lives are oriented toward the endless pursuit of leisure in the suburbs, and we keep hustling and buying instead of accepting the gift of rest we already have in a God who has every resource at his disposal.

> Who knew that drinking the dust of our idols is actually a gift?

But there is good news. There is a better story. First, always first, we must feel how it feels to have bare ears. We must see our hopes catch in our throat as we drink the dust of broken dreams. Who knew that drinking the dust of our idols is actually a gift?

FAILURE, FASTING, AND FEASTING

When Jesus met with the rich young ruler, the young man had done all the right things, followed the religious laws. So he asked Jesus what any good religious student who wants to do well should ask, "What must I do to have eternal life?" Rather than doling out more rules, Jesus pauses. Beautifully, before answering, Matthew writes that Jesus looked at the young man and loved him. Jesus then tells him to sell all he has, give to the poor, and come and follow Jesus. Famously, the young man goes away sad "because he had great wealth" (Mark 10:22 NIV). Jesus saw. Then Jesus loved.

It was out of Jesus' great love for the man that he longed to unsaddle him from the weight of his wealth. It is not that money or wealth is unequivocally bad (though Jesus did say it was hard for the rich to enter the kingdom of heaven), but that his heart was in the grip of his wealth. Like a bit in a horse's mouth, wealth directed him. The man's wealth was the millstone around his neck, the thing he served more than God. And like all false gods—from golden calves to a Target haul—when we find worth by our affluence, it promises rest but brings stress, increasing demands, and a greater devotion to a god that will never love us and always forsake us.

Do you long to feel unburdened by your stuff? Do you desire space to breathe so you could truly enjoy your family, friends, and neighbors? What would it be like to begin to imagine how you could creatively meet the needs of those around you? But when our closets, hearts, minds, and wallets are stuffed to the gills, there is no room to move toward others. So, what can we do now? As we use our spaces for others rather than ourselves, we push back against consumerism. Let's consider a few starting places or counterliturgies to push against our proclivities to use people, places, and things as objects of our consumption.

We must reacquaint ourselves with failure. We're experts at passing the buck and blaming our circumstances when we fail to measure up. We often move away from the people, places, and things that trigger our failures. We think a new lover, a new house, a new neighborhood or city will satisfy. Rather than running away, when we are forced to stare our failures in the face, we may pause long enough to long for and head toward home like the prodigal.

For example, in the middle of a recent marital spat, I flung angry, completely irrelevant words at my husband. Because I felt hurt, I aired dirty laundry, accused, stomped, and railed. It was not my finest moment. But after the tornado had passed, my husband said these words that stopped me in my tracks: "You are mine. I love you. You need to repent, but that doesn't mean that I don't love you. Ashley, I'm asking you to repent because I love you. And [the most gorgeous words in the universe] I'm not going anywhere." My husband wanted more than rightness for me. His anger didn't wall me out, it pulled me toward him. He saw me flailing my arms, trying to take up space, trying to be someone, even using sin to be seen, and he loved me. But love can only be built when we reckon with our failure, when we practice repentance. Love can grow only when our stories are not focused on ourselves but when they move toward the other (even when hurting) and offer to take off the burden of all the golden calves we're shackled to.

Failure is a gift. When we are forced to drink the dust of our idols, we can begin to turn our sights toward home. It is a gift when we run into the places where they cease to satisfy. We fight with our spouses. Our children don't perform. Our job hijacks our time and fails to capture our affections. We suffer from depression, anxiety, and trying to wrestle a family schedule, all the while wondering what we do so much driving for. Success, esteem, good work to do, sharing food with others on your granite countertops, all point to the weight of glory that mere objects cannot hold. And when the objects break, when you lose your job, when your wife gets ill, when relationships are rocky, it all crumbles like the dust it is.

To practice counterliturgies to consumerism, we must also learn the rhythms of fasting and feasting. In a wonderful book on technology usage, Andy Crouch writes, "of course we are meant to eat, and even to feast, but only when we *fast* do we make real progress toward being free of our dependence on food to soothe our depression and anesthetize our anxieties." In other words, we need to hold fasting and feasting together; each only makes sense alongside the other.

We must create times to fast from a lifestyle of affluence we've become accustomed to. If we are to find holy in the suburbs, we must detach from stuff, but not in the sense that the material doesn't matter. God after all called his created order good, and deigned to come save us through his human body. And not in the sense that we are already detached from the forms of production, where we don't know the human cost of our cheap toys and clothes. Rather, we must see how, as Cavanaugh writes, "Things are not ends in themselves; they are means to greater attachment to others. . . . But to have a good relationship with others, it is necessary to have a proper relationship with things." We do this by fasting.

Some ideas are explored at the end of this chapter, but fasting from consumerism might look like putting your phone down, not buying something just because you can, interrogating your heart about your vacations and your granite countertop kitchen remodel. Because if the story of Jesus is true, then it means that, as Abraham Kuyper said, "every square inch" is under the lordship of Christ. If he is Lord, he is Lord over your stuff too. And because he loves you, like he loved the rich young man, he longs for us to be free—to take the heavy weight of consumerism off our chests and give us abundant life.

We must feast well too—which means loving people for who they are, enjoying our things for what they are and not the dreams they promise. May we not turn our families, homes, neighbors, strangers who produce products we consume, or communities into commodities to be bought and sold.

Our stuff must find its proper place—not as signifying objects but as harbingers of another world. C. S. Lewis writes, "They are only the scent of a flower we have not found, the echo of a tune we have not heard, news from a country we have never yet visited." Our good golden objects are pictures that foreshadow glory. They tell us a true tale where we will one day be home in a place of rest, peace, and belonging. They are appetizers of the feast, but not the feast itself. We are not to gorge our bodies, minds, efforts, and hearts on mere nouns.

As we practice counterliturgies to consumerism, we ask for hearts that are not content with the thing itself but hunger for the source of our desires. We sit in this uncomfortable space as we realize how we have been more formed by a liturgy of consumerism than by the Word of God. When we step back and see how we've used our money in ways that are antithetical to what we say is in our hearts—that we've been worshiping a golden calf next to the altar of God—may we search desperately for rescue.

For now let's sit and feel our ears bare. May the dust of our idols catch in our throats and awake us to our deathly habits of consumption. For it is there—in the pulverizing of our golden objects, the bitterness of drinking it down—that grace starts in the suburbs.

COUNTERLITURGIES

to Consumerism ←

Consider these as starting points: a few practices to help shape your habits away from consuming people, places, or things.

1. *Failure.* Practice praying a historic prayer of confession to help reacquaint you with a healthy understanding of sin, confession, and repentance.

2. *Feast.* Surround yourself with things that you love. Enjoy great food and drink and focus your time on others as you enjoy. Plan times of feasting in your schedule rather than just getting by.

3. *Fast.* Practice removing yourself regularly from sites of consumerism—where you're tempted to consume things, people, or experiences (the mall, ads on TV, your favorite stores, social media). Instead take up the practice of writing down a gratitude list. Clear out your closet. Donate your stuff or find friends who would appreciate the things that gather dust in your home. Make a plan for how you engage with social media.

4. *Dare yourself to live on less.* Shop your closet instead of buying more. Save what you'd spend going out for a month and give someone an anonymous gift. Sponsor a child. Generosity begets generosity.

5. *Tithe your time.* Evaluate your schedule and ask why you do the voluntary things on your list. Schedule a block of time to help someone out, to spend uninterrupted and undistracted time with your family, and to be outside to meet your neighbors.

2

When Your Worth Is Measured
in Square Footage

INDIVIDUALISM

*Individualism at first dries up only the source of public
virtues, but, in the long run, it attacks and destroys
all the others and is finally absorbed into egoism.*

ALEXIS DE TOCQUEVILLE, *DEMOCRACY IN AMERICA*

WE WALKED INTO ANOTHER LARGE SUBURBAN HOME in our
neighborhood, this time celebrating the soccer season for our four- to
five-year-old sons. Throughout the season, we'd chatted occasionally
with parents, but mostly I giggled at the cute antics of little boys trying
to play the game. "Season" seemed too official of a word for what they'd
done, which was mainly moving in a pack: one kid kicking the ball to
the goal and the others trailing along beside. While we were lucky to
get our family of six to all their games on time, other parents, including the team mom, ran up and down the sidelines videotaping her
son's goals. Whereas I felt like a hot mess, she was organized, on top
of it, and enthusiastic.

We went to the end-of-the-season party mostly because we were
excited for an easy Saturday night: pizza and fun for our four children,
no cleanup, and then straight home to bed. When we arrived, I looked
around, feeling a bit out of place. The men were laughing, already
drinking beers in the kitchen, wearing similar golf polo shirts tucked
into khaki shorts, their hair perfectly combed. As our children grabbed

juices from coolers in the backyard and pounced on all the new toys, my husband and I grabbed a drink, found a spot on the outskirts of the group, and attempted to make conversation with people we didn't really know.

For a while we chatted with a couple who'd moved from the East Coast and loved it in Southern California. My husband then went to talk to some of the men, and I went to say thank you to the hostess. Making polite conversation and asking what she did for a living, I found out both she and her husband were FBI agents. I'd surely walked into a movie—a husband and wife team, living the good life in suburbia, who call their nanny at a moment's notice when they need to catch some bad guys. I had lots of questions but no way to relate.

The team mom, always in a black sundress and large sunglasses, came over. She and FBI Mom knew one another. I thanked Team Mom for her organization. She launched into a rundown of their schedule—how her kids are involved in sports and what after-school programs they do. Because she's an executive who flies around the world every other week, she's become an expert at managing the family schedule. It just made sense to extend it to her son's soccer team. I looked down at my cute shoes and necklace. I was just excited we showed up on time and I wasn't in workout gear. My schedule was on sticky notes taped to the wall in my kitchen.

She had just flown in from meetings in Japan, run home, and volunteered in her child's class. She was really hoping to find a good cleaning service for their four-thousand-square-foot home. She talked about their renovation plans.

I realized, of course, that part of her organizational superhero skills stemmed from the chaos of her life and needing to make sure the children were fed, at school, and attended their activities while she traveled for work. She felt guilty for traveling. Rather than moving toward her, envy twisted in my heart. The way she seemed to do it all. She could wear real clothes and do what felt like important things.

That she could even have her own seat on an airplane without packing fruit snacks and goldfish. That Team Mom and FBI Mom had so much space in their homes.

And then, they asked, what did I do?

I told myself it's okay for people to have more than me. But envy for what seemed a more extraordinary life—and even a larger house—made me insecure. I pulled out my trump card: "Oh," I said, "I have a PhD. We lived in Scotland."

My education and living overseas were my lynchpin. A PhD would show I'm smart and valuable. Living in Scotland would show I was cultured and more than a tourist. These would hold me together and keep me from spinning out of control in the suburbs filled with world travel and large houses we couldn't afford. But it still didn't feel like enough. Really, I wanted the house. Not just because I wanted more space—more than that, I wanted to belong too.

THE STORY OF A HOUSE

Perhaps there is no object more desired than a house in America. Meghan Daum writes in her hilarious and poignant book *Life Would Be Perfect If I Lived in That House*, "There is no object of desire quite like a house. Few things . . . are capable of eliciting such urgent, even painful, yearning." We long for a house as a marker of who we are. Socially a house is evidence of our success and achievement of the American dream. Houses substantiate our financial status, reputation, and taste.

The story of the suburbs is the story of a house. The single-family residence held out an answer to universal hungers for safety, shelter, beauty, and ease. As the suburbs grew in the twentieth century, they provided access to a more affordable house for consumers. Yet increasingly this was only affordable for white, upwardly mobile, and middle-class residents.

In an article in the *New York Times Magazine*, Matthew Desmond reports, "America's national housing policy gives affluent homeowners large benefits; middle-class homeowners, smaller benefits; and most renters, who are disproportionately poor, nothing. It is difficult to think of another social policy that more successfully multiplies America's inequality in such a sweeping fashion." A story in the *Atlantic* states that home ownership remains financially prohibitive if you're not white: "Hispanic Americans are 78 percent more likely to be given a high-cost mortgage and black Americans are 105 percent more likely." Our houses, our neighborhoods, our suburbs are more often than not built to keep people out, rather than welcome people in—and once we have wealth, we like to keep our investments safe by monitoring boundaries of race and class in our neighborhoods.

When we try to find ourselves in a product only available to a select few, we miss out on finding both the kingdom of God and ourselves. Ultimately, because a house remains ultimately "eminently chaseable," as the chief object of our desires, we equate rootedness, safety, and shelter with an object that money can buy.

We answer our hunger for home and belonging with a house. In the suburbs, the bigger (or fancier or more unique) the better. Our worth is measured in square footage.

Houses indeed seem to be human—the way they hold our baggage, carry our pain, and shelter what is most dear to us. Houses are more than mere objects, more than status symbols, more than indicators of class and privilege. We hope, of course, to find

> **Our worth is measured in square footage.**

home in them. But we also hope to find ourselves. The sovereign self is inextricably linked to the house.

Our houses symbolize us—not simply in our decorating choices, but also how they represent us as the "sovereign chooser." In our homes, *we* choose. It is our money, our time, our decor, our values, and even our choices about who does the dishwashing, whether we eat dinner in front of the TV, or even if we eat together. Our practices of home and the stuff of home illustrate what we value. For most of us in the suburbs, we ultimately value ourselves.

IT REALLY IS ALL ABOUT ME

If the suburbs marry the self with the house, this has drastic implications for life lived well in community. Wendell Berry's essay "Sex, Economy, Freedom, and Community" is helpful here. In it, he describes how local communities are attacked from the ambitions of both private and public life. In Berry's terms, a community is rooted in proximity: it is a conglomeration of households and based on the trust gained through mutual, face-to-face interaction. The public, in contrast, focuses on the individual. He writes perceptively of our cultural moment—and describes the choice for suburbanites:

> The individual, unlike the household and the community, always has two ways to turn: she or he may either turn toward the household and the community, to receive membership and to give service, or toward the relatively unconditional life of the public, in which one is free to pursue self-realization, self-aggrandizement, self-interest, self-enrichment, self-promotion, and so on. . . . The individual life implies no standard of behavior or responsibility.

The suburbs cultivate this public life where individuals pursue self-interest and self-promotion, all under the guise of community. We're next to each other, but we're lonely. We close our garages, behind which we pursue our own stories of self-realization; we move out into the world not face-to-face but in cars, windows up, ready to consume the next activity. We emerge from our garages for neighborly gestures, but life is not lived there, between neighbors.

In the suburbs we like the sheen of community, but real community is messy and unkempt. Instead, we center ourselves so our stories revolve around us. Whether these stories focus on granite countertops and exotic vacations, or on yoga and green juice, whether they take the form of intellectual growth or Christian service to others, they all repeat the chorus: me, me, me.

In a life lived for the self, people easily morph into products. We jump to "what can they do for me?" when we meet someone. We make our places the backdrop to a story where we are the heroes. We imagine freedom as a life of no constraints, where we're free to pursue our dreams (we've been told it all growing up)—whether we're buying them, working hard for them by climbing corporate ladders, or even digging into our souls. Each path is another way up the mountain of self-actualization. The "stay true to yourself" mantra, when it is not grounded in deep, sacrificial community, simply baptizes our selfishness. Self-actualization is a dead end that leaves us lonely.

There's also a particularly Christian version of the self-actualization narrative: it's found in hearing how the salvation story revolved around me and God's wonderful plan for my life. This story wound its way around us so that mission trips were validations for the goodness of a soul. It grew a vocabulary around a person's seriousness about living for Jesus, and a subsequent call to "change the world" by doing big, exotic things. This story found a liturgy in the hours of personal Bible study and puritanical evaluation of the dark nights of the soul. It's not that these activities are wrong but that Christian piety, belief, and practice continue to be wrapped up in a narrative of the self, where the *I* is the key to unlocking faith. God does have a wonderful plan for your life, but blessedly that is not the point.

Redemption is not, in fact, all about you. Freedom is not about you at all. It is not a freedom *from*—an "escape from the constraints of community" (Berry again)—but a freedom *for*. Freedom is a far grander story than a suburban bootstrapperism, where your worth is measured in square footage.

As Mike Wilkerson writes in his book *Redemption*, "If your story of redemption stops at your healing or your freedom, then you do not yet have God's vision for redemption." We need a story that is as good as it is true, as outrageous and merciful as it is fierce, as compassionate and encompassing as it is intimate. We need a story of redemption that can accomplish the shalom of the entire cosmos.

Wilkerson continues, God "wants to do something in you, yes; but beyond that, he wants to do something through you. He wants to make his name known." If the real story of redemption is not just of souls but also of all things, as a proclamation of the glory of God himself, then we need more than simplistic faith formulas to find holy in the suburbs. We need more than get-out-of-hell salvation for individual souls. We desperately need the kingdom of God to break through individualism, the birthright of suburban living, and consumerism, its favorite mode.

> We desperately need the kingdom of God to break through individualism, the birthright of suburban living, and consumerism, its favorite mode.

Only then will we want to work for our neighborhoods by "aligning [ourselves] with the grain of [our] place and answering to its needs." But I can never answer the needs of my neighborhood when I'm telling a story that has *me* at the center instead of *us*, and when home is a product of what I buy, and when worth is measured in square footage.

MY HOME IS MY (SAND)CASTLE

When we first moved back to the suburbs, at first I found myself repulsed by the trappings of consumerism and then strangely fascinated by it. Until, after a few months, I realized I wanted the best that it had to offer: a home of my own.

There was a period of months when instead of scrolling through Facebook, Twitter, or Instagram, I obsessively watched the housing app Zillow. When we moved home to the suburbs I was shocked at the sticker price for tract homes that were still ten miles from the ocean. To purchase a home the same size as our home in Salt Lake City would cost triple in the Southern California suburbs. But the price tag didn't stop my yearning.

In the quiet as my children napped, I'd scroll through Zillow evaluating square footage, bedrooms, and floor plans to see if there was a postage-stamp-size yard or not. We'd spend weekends telling our children to not jump on the beds while at model home tours. I reasoned with God that our life as church planters and the parents of four children warranted more space. How were we supposed to be hospitable, God, when it's hard to cram in thirty people for a church meeting in our rented home? How are we supposed to show the goodness of God and his kingdom, I wondered, if we didn't have ample space to be generous? Couldn't just one thing in our lives feel a bit easy, God? Didn't we deserve a house with four bedrooms?

In my suburban walks, I'd catch myself walking by larger homes, modern versions of a California mission style or ones that looked like they belonged in an East Coast fishing village. Like our modern-day propensity to reach for our phones when our hearts are sad, confused, or lonely, I kept scrolling through Zillow as an automatic reaction during my children's nap times. Surely, I reasoned, we'd get a cash windfall or we'd find a short sale, and I needed to know what's out there. I used Scripture to justify my addiction: God didn't, after all, call us into the wilderness to starve us, I reckoned. It's good and right to desire to stay and put down roots whether you're in the suburbs, city, or small town—but this wasn't that.

I scrolled through Zillow because I measured my worth by square footage. The desire for home and to be committed to the community we're called to serve looked like property values, the number of bedrooms, and space to entertain—not as status symbols or more stuff to accumulate. It's what the square footage stood for. I just wanted space.

I wanted space for quiet and to be undisturbed. I wanted a bit more of a buffer between my neighbors and myself so I didn't have to worry about my children hitting someone's house with a soccer ball. I wanted space to move away from the pain of conflict that occurs when living in community. I wanted more space because I wanted more me and less of the hard work of actually creating community in all its painful glory. So in a classic act of blame-shifting that's been kin to us since the Garden, I thought that moving place would solve the problems of community. I'd find somewhere where I could be autonomous. I wanted a house to change my heart, to calm my soul's restlessness.

When I kept scrolling through Zillow, I didn't want a house that intimately involved me in the life of my neighbors; I wanted something built to suit only my own desires. I wanted a glorious sandcastle.

SUBURBAN EXILES

It is not that owning a house (even a large one) is necessarily wrong, but rather that more often than not our sense of self expands to fit our homes—bigger house, bigger self. When our selves are so big, we cannot live in vulnerable, hospitable community. On this side of the Garden, we must be weaned from ourselves. Exile is often God's gracious way to bring us home to himself. Yet, as a character in Graham Greene's novel *The End of the Affair* puts it, "It's such an odd sort of mercy, it sometimes looks like punishment."

The Bible has a rich history of our covenant-making God who woos his people, calls them by name, and calls them to follow him. In the Old Testament we see cycles where God's people commit themselves to God, but then become enamored with the gods of the culture surrounding them (remember that golden calf). God then disciplines his wayward children; they often repent and are restored, only to again fall into sin. The pattern of exile and redemption is one way to understand the physical and spiritual consequences of sin. We choose our gods, and at times they are ground up and we must drink them. That is the odd sort of God's mercy.

But oftentimes exile doesn't look as flashy as the golden calf at the base of Mount Sinai under the thundering power of God. Sometimes we can relive the pattern of exile right at home, at the end of our cul-de-sac, doing all the right things. We can rebel spectacularly by repudiating God's goodness, wishing he were dead, and dividing up the spoils in a far-off country. Or, like the elder brother in the parable of the prodigal son, we can also live at home, do what's right, and present an outward show of perfect obedience. Meanwhile, we're biding our time, waiting for the old man to die so we can get what's coming to us. Both are manifestations of our spiritual exile—that we're not at home. Exile isn't only about physical distance. Exile may not simply be discipline for sin, an outward sign of our spiritual homelessness; it's also a state of the heart. Whatever its form, rebellion is traveling away from God, who is our home and our promised land.

The language of exile, of "resident aliens," of being strangers in a strange land, spawned a bunch of bad Christian bumper stickers and T-shirts in the United States in the 1990s. Then, a sense of Christian identity meant that "being in the world but not of it" more often meant withdrawing from society (see John 17:16). It meant that we could live as an enclave of moral do-gooders, looking forward to getting raptured into heaven. The mission then for us in the evangelicalism of the 1990s was to save souls out of this world, to do "big things for God," to remain sexually pure and morally good.

What I didn't know as a teenager then was that you can do all the right things and still be far from the heart of God. We can stew in bitterness and resentment thinking God owes us more than himself. We don't want him; we just want his stuff—whether that's a cute boyfriend, the flashiest car, the college acceptance letter, the influential job, or the suburban house.

What that version of faith taught suburban teenagers like me is that because "this world is not my home," we could chuck it and withdraw, or we could acquiesce to the gods of culture. There was no third way that I knew of. I didn't have a vocabulary of cultural renewal, of God being intimately concerned with how and why I could read something like Lolita or Hume or Nietzsche, and what it meant to my faith.

The tendency of exile is either to fully assimilate into the conquering culture (buy the nicest house) or create workable subcultures, like my Christian one of pious living. In exile, it's easy to believe what the empire tells us: that we are home now, that the powers that be (whether they are the gods of the marketplace or of a nation) hold the key to security and well-being, and that we needn't live on the threshold between the kingdom of God being "already here" but "not yet" fully arrived.

◦ ☁ ☀ ☁ ◦

When God's people were taken captive in Babylon, the psalmist writes of his experience in Psalm 137:

> By the waters of Babylon,
>   there we sat down and wept,
>   when we remembered Zion.
> On the willows there
>   we hung up our lyres.
> For there our captors
>   required of us songs,
> and our tormentors, mirth, saying,
>   "Sing us one of the songs of Zion!"
> How shall we sing the LORD's song
>   in a foreign land? (Psalm 137:1-4)

If we are separated and cut off from God—exiled—because of sin, will we continue doing moral things, following the forms of upright living that are as flimsy as 1990s bumper stickers? Or will we be changed?

Will the forms of our faith be laughable relics to the wielders of power when they are so watered down? Will we measure ourselves by our square footage and keep buttressing our own selves, or will we learn the lessons of exile? Will we learn how to practice lament and vulnerability? Can we learn to sing truth to the powers of consumerism and individualism that hold us in their grasp?

THE GIFT OF EXILE

If we hunger for home, but the suburban way is to feed that hunger with square footage, our experience of exile offers a counterliturgy. Exile, it turns out, has a surprising gift tucked inside: our exile points back to the promise of a home. It's a better one than any I found through Zillow.

In Isaiah 40, the prophet speaks words of comfort to God's people in exile. "Comfort, comfort my people," he writes. "Speak tenderly to Jerusalem" because "her iniquity is pardoned, / that she has received from the LORD's hand / double for all her sins" (Isaiah 40:1-2). Not that Jerusalem has received a double punishment, but that she has received a double pardon. It is not simply that salvation in Jesus means that our sins are forgiven and we are left at ground zero, but more than that: we are also given Christ's righteousness. We are given a double portion. Because Jesus knew exile, we have a home. Because Jesus knew and experienced exile, our own times of exile are not devoid of God's presence. Because Jesus was rejected and forsaken, we can be the lambs he tenderly gathers like a shepherd.

In the suburbs, it's easy to become numb to the ways we pursue our own self-satisfaction—whether it's through our physical house or it's packaged as abstract nouns. All these abstract nouns (like *success, meaning, purpose,* and *self-esteem*) are contingent on the kingdom of self. They are versions of Wendell Berry's "relatively unconditional life of the public," and they masquerade as freedom. But we need physical and even spiritual wilderness moments to bring us home. We need the prick of exile to see how far we've traveled, even when we've done all the right things and live cozily wrapped up in our suburban homes.

Yes, it's much safer for us to politely wave to the man across the street, perhaps engage in courteous small talk, and shut our garage doors. It's easier to build up the kingdom of self while neglecting the local and particular challenges of proximity. But I want so much more for the suburbs than individualism. God is a God who sees. He gathers his flock, he speaks tenderly, and he sees the outcast. He is near to the brokenhearted. The proud suburbanites, though, he may need to humble. That too is his mercy. That is the gift of exile. The gift of exile means that someone hasn't given up on you or felt you are not worth pursuing.

It's like a parent who uses whole food to wean their child from sugar addiction and a proclivity for Cheetos. There is, of course, the inevitable sugar crash. Exile too means even when you stuff yourself full of things meant to satisfy your cravings for beauty, meaning, and significance, God still sees and he comes down. He gives us whole food. It means that all your longings you prop up with your square footage are actually seen, known, and sympathized with. It means there is a home for all your longings. It means there is rest for the weary.

> **The gift of exile means that someone hasn't given up on you or felt you are not worth pursuing.**

The good news of the gospel often blows through in exile. We must be "moved by the signs of what it cost to bring [us] home." This smarts a bit and wounds our pride as we peel back the layers and find ourselves needy, wanting, and inconsequential. Because no matter one's income bracket, suffering, loss, and longing are no respecter of persons. But the gift of exile is both that God comes near to the suffering, right in our weakness (2 Corinthians 12:10), and exile will always point us home.

In *Orthodoxy* G. K. Chesterton writes of his conversion and his first understanding of sin. He writes, "I had tried to be happy by telling myself that man is an animal," yet it only brought sadness rather than relief because it did not satisfy. The optimist's perspective on human nature felt too naive, while the pessimist's perspective appeared too bleak. But upon experiencing this sense of being both made in God's image and shattered by sin, Chesterson rejoiced, for he reckons he "had been right in feeling all things as odd, for I myself was at once worse and better than all things." That is, as we hold in tension both creation and the fall, we feel hung in the balance. We are homesick even in our suburban houses. Experiencing existential exile, even in the suburbs, is a gift because it points to our shared human homesickness.

And if we are homesick even at home, it means that our glorious sandcastles will never satisfy no matter how nice they are or how much space they have for doing good works. We will always be homesick no matter our square footage when we use our square footage to buttress the kingdom of self.

There is only one place we can go where we will find home and get relief from the constant reiteration of ourselves. There is only one place where we can enjoy blessed self-forgetfulness, and nothing in the suburbs (or city or country) will ever satisfy. We can only go to the "rock that does not move" where God, who has gone through exile on our behalf, will show himself ever, always, and tenderly steadfast.

COUNTERLITURGIES

to Individualism ←

1. *Get outside.* Practice noticing the natural world around you. What do you touch, see, smell, and hear? What does the natural world have to teach you about your place in it?

2. *Get outside yourself.* Begin imagining what practices you could take up that move you toward other people. Schedule thirty minutes to be available to your neighborhood. Notice its needs. Introduce yourself to a neighbor.

3. *Notice what you complain about.* Whether it's the insidiousness of laundry, a bad driver, or the demands on your time, notice how what you complain about centers on yourself.

4. *Downsize and upsize.* Downsize your stuff, your schedule, maybe even your house. Take up new practices that increase not yourself but the story of God. Practice a small habit like reading a psalm daily, waking up and praying a prayer of gratitude before your feet hit the floor, and staying quiet to listen to God and other people.

3

Circling the Suburbs in My Minivan

BUSYNESS

Our controlled frenzy creates the illusion of a well-ordered existence. We move from crisis to crisis, responding to the urgent and neglecting the essential.

BRENNAN MANNING, *ABBA'S CHILD*

I TOOK DEEP BREATHS. On little pink sticky notes, I again wrote my boys' soccer practice schedule—hoping that the more I wrote it, the less frantic the schedule would actually become. It said:

Drop off Porter at 4
Drop off Camden at 5
Drop Ezra early at 5:25
Pick up Porter at 5:30
Home to prep dinner
Pick up Camden at 6
Eat dinner
Pick up Ezra at 6:45
Homework, Showers, Bed

It was dizzying. *Was I going to be in my minivan for two straight hours? How were we going to do homework? Should I drive through McDonald's at half hour intervals to get them all fed instead of cooking?* If we took the McDonald's route, I reasoned, I'd be stuck in the car with my three-year-old daughter, Harriet, strapped into her car seat, but I could catch up on podcasts and talk to friends, while also feeding all four children, and get everyone where they needed to be on time. I might even be able to help with homework as we circled the suburbs in my minivan. I imagined treating myself to a latte at the drive-through Starbucks right next to McDonald's.

It seemed like the supermom plan: stay in the car, go through as many drive-throughs as possible, and get all the things done. But I also felt guilty imagining feeding my children fake chicken nuggets. I'd watched the YouTube videos about what really happened at fast-food restaurants, and if I fed them that, did I even love my children? I felt guilty for putting miles on the car. I felt guilty because this was not the life I wanted to live, circling the suburbs on a Monday afternoon. I wanted meaning, depth, connection; a life of drive-throughs and sports practices didn't feel like the abundant life. It just felt too busy.

Yet how were we supposed to do all the things—get everyone where they needed to go; finish homework; feed my kids a dinner they'd eat but one that was also nutritious and not filled with food dye or weird chemical additives; not have too much screen time; help my children develop into kind, respectful, responsible people who were compassionate and did things like brush their teeth and change their underwear without being asked; and also create meaningful con-nection and a lifetime of memories as a family? I was exhausted just thinking about it, and I hadn't even got to all the other stuff—like have a relationship with God, read my Bible, love my neighbors, go to church, and serve the poor.

So instead of McDonald's I ran home in thirty-minute increments to serve up what my children call "snacky dinner": our plates piled with salami, bread, apples, cheese, eggs, olives, and a veggie or two we had on hand. At least I'd checked off the nutritional box on my mom list. But my soul was still frantic. Healthy food hadn't solved the problem. It wasn't just a problem with our time or our minivan. It was a deeper problem of my heart. How we spend our time—like how we spend our money—shows where our hearts are. I was hurrying to check off boxes to be a "good mom," but I wasn't resting in who God said I was. I couldn't do all the things. Certainly busyness wasn't the answer to a more abundant life. But I was in too deep. How could I find rest— more than that, how could I find God—when I spend my time circling the suburbs?

A DESIRE FOR WORK AND REST

It took me about a week to recover from that Monday when I religiously followed my pickup and drop-off list, and tried to put dinner on the table. I know most of us circle the suburbs in our minivans or sit in traffic after work, and that sometimes a full schedule is inevitable. But for most of us in middle-class suburban America, being busy is a status marker, where "the shift from leisure-as-status to busyness-as-status may be linked to the development of knowledge-intensive economies." Because in the suburbs most of us work in this knowledge economy, we've lost obvious external markers of a job well done. Most of us don't see progress in crops harvested or in building a piece of furniture, where we put in effort, grow our skills, and complete projects. Now, we can work 24/7.

In a knowledge-based economy, the way we make ourselves seen and even validated is through more work. Busyness shows us that we're valuable, contributing members to society. So whether we can't stop checking our email or driving our children around to every extra-curricular activity in the suburbs, we've equated our busyness with value. Because our Western culture values work as an "essential element of identity," we stay busy to stay valuable.

We all crave real rest. I'm still trying to re-create the tightly pulled white sheets of my grandmother's guest bed, the feel of the fluffy comforter tightly tucked under my chin—not just in down duvet but in a feeling of warm safety, where things have their place. Her home was clean, cozy, and perfectly at ease with itself (in contrast to my own home, which often feels like it's chaotically spinning out of control). But beyond a nicely made bed, we hunger to maintain a level of rest borne from good, hard, satisfying work—one that is filled not with mind-numbingly flipping television channels but a soul rest that refuels us toward "love and good works" (Hebrews 10:24). We want the rest that the Bible promises—we want sabbath.

We hunger for time that is marked and noticed, not simply checked off our pink sticky notes. We want to know that someone else has created, toiled, and worked, and the weight of the world is not on our shoulders. We can sit down in gratitude. We are not responsible for much. The world will keep on spinning. We are held in the gaze of a God who not only created the cosmos but also numbers the hairs on our heads. We, like a small child, need not eat "the bread of anxious toil" (Psalm 127:2) but instead trust that our Father will meet all our needs in Christ Jesus.

In the suburbs we accrue fast-food fixes to our deep soul hungers. When we're hungry, we often keep doing laps around the drive-through in a fit of rush and hurry. But we are often left with meals that do not satisfy, with plastic toys that break, and the smell of French fries that won't leave our minivans. So it is with our souls. We settle for the quick route to satiation, the fast-food gods of the suburbs such as busyness, and then find ourselves with a stomachache in the bathroom.

Rather than practicing the rest we crave, rather than living out of a storehouse of belovedness, rather than confessing our sin, we substitute leisure for rest. Surely the vacation (or the weight loss, or my children's success, or my promotion, or my granite countertops, or even all my volunteer activities and an obsession with coconut oil) will satisfy. We measure "the good life" in miles driven, productivity hacks, and checking off our to-do lists. We slow down long enough so we can check out and then again serve the machine. So when leisure doesn't satisfy, we keep on the go. By staying busy, we imagine our movement will save us.

We spend the equivalent of seven forty-hour work weeks on average in our cars in America. We pick up takeout or have it delivered—all to save time,

> By staying busy, we imagine our movement will save us.

which seems to move ever faster, eluding capture. We lose something in our constant movement.

In her book on the Jewish practice of sabbath, Judith Shulevitz writes, "People began to learn, first from the telegraph, then from radio, newsreels, television, and the Internet, that what was happening *now*, all over the globe, mattered more than what was happening *here*." That is, it is not only the technology we use but also our means of transportation, our daily habits, which change our orientation from being present, embodied, and emplaced people to trying to be everywhere at the same time.

Our schedules and routes are not ruled by God's kingdom but by the shifting sands of what constitutes success. Masters at transforming God's gift of time into a commodity so we can control it, we have made "saving time" our favorite way to live. A focus on ease, leisure, and even all the ways we try to be increasingly efficient is another way to follow the siren call of the suburban gods instead of a God who calls us out of hiding. What are we even saving our time for?

Moving from busyness to unfettered leisure never brings restorative rest. The liturgy of busyness does not save us; it does not stave off anxiety, sadness, or insure financial success. It springs up from a well of worry, a deep-seated feeling that we must ceaselessly work to take care of ourselves and our children. What begins as a protective impulse morphs into the tail wagging the dog: we are run by our schedules, by our too-full calendar, and by extending a story of self rather than joining in what and how God is already at work. When there is no space in our schedules to meet with God's people or open our homes to others, we cannot expect our deep hungers to be filled.

When we can't be still, we'll simply keep circling the suburbs, trying to find the essential but always chasing the urgent.

GOD OF ABUNDANCE IN THE DESOLATE SPOT

Underneath our frantic pace is a question: Is this work I do good enough? Am *I* good enough? And perhaps for those who were wannabe world changers, we feel guilty for our suburban life. We don't yet know in our bones how we can live right and love well at the end of our cul-de-sacs, so we busy ourselves trying to find meaning, significance, and value in frenzied activity. But speeding up life never satisfies our hungers. Scripture promises again and again we will be satisfied—not with more to do but with God himself.

A cursory reading of the Gospels shows Jesus walking across Galilee feeding thousands of people at a time. At least once a week, we read

> Scripture promises again and again we will be satisfied—not with more to do but with God himself.

my daughter's children's story Bible and marvel at the child offering his loaves and fishes to the Son of God, how Jesus' disciples gathered baskets upon baskets of leftovers, and no one needed to eat another bite. But before Jesus fed the five thousand, he was trying to get away.

He'd sent his disciples out to heal disease and preach the good news of repentance, and they returned minicelebrities—so much so that everyone who needed help came to them. The disciples couldn't even eat.

Jesus holds out the promise of rest when he tells them: "Come away by yourselves to a desolate place and rest a while" (Mark 6:31). They've been faithful, God has shown up, they've seen miracles and repentance, and now they just want to be with Jesus. The landscape they travel to matches their internal state—they need quiet, calm, and a filling of all the worn-out, desolate spots of themselves too.

But when they get to the desolate spot, a crowd has run ahead of them. Then, in the text, we're met with this beautiful sentence: "When [Jesus] went ashore he saw a great crowd, and he had compassion on them, because they were like sheep without a shepherd" (Mark 6:34).

The few times I've been around sheep (and that's not much, given my suburban life and flirtation with worldwide cities), they've been smelly, oblivious creatures wandering across Scottish country lanes. They're not much to look at. Jesus and his disciples are tired and worn out, just wanting to get away, and they're presented with a crowd of stinky, desperate-looking creatures. While his disciples may have been angrily disappointed, Jesus' compassion is aroused even in his weariness.

Later, after Jesus has spent time teaching, the disciples are still looking for their plans to be fulfilled the way they'd hoped: they wanted Jesus all to themselves. They craved rest within the boundaries of their plan—send the people away to eat. They can figure out how to meet their own needs. The disciples surely weren't responsible for anyone. Yet Jesus says they are. He puts the need for food right back into the disciples' laps by asking them to feed the people—not to see who could come up with the most creative plan but for them to realize what we need to know too: we never feed ourselves, and we are always responsible for one another.

After complaining about the prohibitive cost of feeding so many people, the disciples follow his command to "go and see" what's available and come back with five loaves and two fish. Jesus depends on his Father to provide food as he looks to heaven, and the loaves and fishes are miraculously multiplied. He gives them to his disciples to distribute so they feel the heft of abundance in their hands and baskets. As their true Shepherd, Jesus provides, lets his sheep dwell in safety, and feeds them.

When the Israelites wandered the desert, God met their hungers with manna. When Moses complains to God about the burden of the people and their desire for meat ("Did I give them birth? . . . Where am I to get meat to give to all this people?" [Numbers 11:12-13]), God provides quail. Our human knee-jerk reaction is to circle the wagons around our plans, to see our days and our time as so scarce that it must be dissected, divvied up, and our plans executed so we can continue on the path to progress. We think we're responsible for providing for ourselves, and we can't begin to imagine manna or quail, or how bread and fish could feed five thousand people. We can't conceive of how our time could be multiplied, that there could be rest after the weary work week. We don't yet have a hunger to see how our time could be used to feed others and not simply parceled out in small mouthfuls so we all have just barely enough.

Like the disciples, we must go to desolate places. But in upwardly mobile, often largely white suburban contexts, we're scared of desert spaces. They don't fit the pattern of the good life. We shy away from discomfort and act like God is our faith multivitamin, but our lives are largely unshaped by the gospel. For anything to shape us, we must commit to the hard desert spaces of unknowing. Marlena Graves writes of these desolate spaces, "All these giants of the faith spent time in the physical desert but were also intimately acquainted with the interior desert. Eventually, God sends all who truly seek to know him into a spiritual wilderness." But instead of trusting in a God who is with us even in the wilderness, in the suburbs we use our busyness to stiff-arm God. We're scared he'll bring us to the desert. If faith in Christ is to be life changing, we can't bend God to our suburban whims—we can't fit him into a life of hurry.

If these wilderness spaces don't find us through tragedy, failure, and loss, we need to seek them out. We need to forcibly remove ourselves from the rat race and allow our souls to flex and breathe. When we go to desolate places (whether that's slowing down enough to be in nature or those desolate places inside of ourselves we find when we stop moving), we're likely to become a bit annoyed like the disciples or angry at God like Moses. Everything we've pushed down in order to be productive will probably bubble up in anger, grief, disappointment, envy, sadness, or confusion. The good news is that the God of the universe can take our "It's not fair" feet-stomping tantrums and sadness. We worship a God who can deal with our disappointment, confusion, doubts, and questions; a God who will be present when we put down our phones or stop driving.

Jesus always, always meets us with himself. There is abundant food for the weary, worn out, and sarcastic among us. Jesus gives the disciples (and us) space to complain when we're met with needs and hungers we can't fulfill on our own. Our deep hungers—for food, rest, or meaningful work—won't be filled by taking time into our hands like fishes and loaves, pulling off tiny pieces, and hoping a small morsel will satisfy. No, the only way is to come empty-handed; to question God, to wrestle with him. When the need is too great, then we have no choice but to be gently led by our compassionate Shepherd. Curled there where his rod and staff comfort us, we find real rest. He sees we do not seem to have enough time, compassion, or resources to provide for ourselves, let alone others. He sees and he provides.

God is never in a hurry. When we rush around, running our lives like a cruise director, we fail to see that our resources, like loaves and fish, are not our

> Our time is a precious gift that will be multiplied only when it is corralled by the good story of the gospel.

own. They were never our own to manage as we saw fit. Our time is not ours to micromanage. Our time is a precious gift that will be multiplied only when it is corralled by the good story of the gospel.

Like loaves and fish, there will be enough. More than enough.

ORDINARY TIME

One evening when reading our dinner devotional book, I read about the Feast of Trumpets, a once-a-year event when the Israelites were called (literally) to repentance. The trumpet would sound and they'd remember that their time was God's gift and whether they'd spent it well or not. Nancy Guthrie writes, "God set up a yearly holiday called the Festival of Trumpets to blast the people out of their spiritual laziness." Sometimes I wish we'd get a trumpet blast to arouse us out of our spiritual stupors, so we'd be forced to see how we use busyness to block our ears.

We need trumpet calls and wake-up calls. We need to say no to the things that lead us away from the story of God and lead us to follow a story of the suburbs. The suburbs keep us busy because we think the more we move, the more we work, the more valuable we will be.

If we hope to nurture a life of faith, we've got to stop moving long enough to hear God's voice.

The gospel says: come to the desolate space. Tantrum, scream, cry, face your fears of insignificance and irrelevancy there. Then find rest in a rest that is not of your own making. Find Jesus. And having found Jesus, we will be sent out, and he will ask us impossible things—not to test us but to show us (even in the food we eat) that he provides not only for our hungers but also for the hunger pains of our communities.

God will be found by us in the desolate spaces. Going to desolate places might look like recalibrating our time to fit what we say we value. It might be removing our phones from our nightstands and choosing to not document our lives on social media. It may be committing to read our Bibles even when we're not sure if God will show up.

Our time is not our own to fill like an empty shopping cart—with whatever strikes our fancy and fits our budget. Our time (like our money) is a means to love God and serve others. Paradoxically, only as we give of our resources will we be filled. This isn't American bootstrapperism where we muscle it out to be generous; instead it's slowing down and acknowledging that we have a Father God who sees our needs and kindly answers them for our good and his good pleasure.

But if our schedules are packed too tight—like our closets—there will never be room to let in anything new, including God. Our daily habits, our weekly schedules, and our purchases all add up to how we spend our lives. Anything we turn to that dictates our daily habits also shapes our hearts. We hunger for good work and restorative rest, and yet we stay busy because we fear we won't find anything in the desolate places. But what if instead of circling the suburbs or distracting ourselves, we simply stopped? What if we said no more often? What would happen if we slowed down?

We could begin to live ordinary time well.

When we live ordinary time well, we practice disciplines that increase our hunger for the right things—not the quick-fix chicken nuggets of the soul, but the nutritious meal. We pray. We read our Bibles. We give. We serve. We partake in the sacraments and dig our hands into the life of the church.

When we live ordinary time well, we choose to spend our time for God's kingdom instead of building up the kingdom of self. When we do, we don't have to force our days, plans, or even our memories to provide total satisfaction. In her book *Simply Tuesday*, Emily P. Freeman writes, "Part of living well in ordinary time is letting *this day* be good. Letting *this day* be a gift. Letting *this day* be filled with plenty. And if it all goes wrong and my work turns to dust? This is my kind reminder that outcomes are beyond the scope of my job description." When we stop moving, we realize time was never our own. Then, our days can be received as gifts.

If we slowed down and pruned our schedules, we'd begin to de-center ourselves. We'd practice sustained attention and even be bored. We could begin to imagine what finding holy in the suburbs would look like in our hearts, families, and neighborhoods. We'd give our children the tools to know how to be comfortable in their own skin without having to perform to feel loved. We'd give them (and us) a better way to live in a culture that says you have to stay busy to be seen. We'd show them a better way to belong than through joining a frenzied, success- and image-driven culture.

The upside-down kingdom of God in the suburbs stakes this claim: you don't have to be busy to belong. When we stop striving, we don't have to hoard our time or treasure. God's kingdom testifies that rest is possible, not just checking out from the rat race in your favorite version of suburban leisure, but more than that, we can experience a deep, restorative rest. The gospel says that in Jesus we're held, protected, loved, and valued simply because we are God's children.

But to imagine a vision larger than what our suburbs sell as success and productivity, we have to have the courage to slow down. There we have the space to wrestle with all that our busyness hides and there, we pray, we will find God.

COUNTERLITURGIES
→ to Busyness

1. *Pray through your calendar.* As you start a new season or new month, pray through your calendar with your family. Prayerfully consider your commitments and what furthers a life of generosity and other-centeredness versus what satisfies your whims.

2. *Say no.* To say the right yeses, we need to say no first and have patience in the waiting. Practice saying no before you automatically say yes with your time.

3. *Make a list of things that feed your soul.* With a list of things that feed your soul, you'll know what things you can prioritize to rest well rather than get sucked into what your suburb says is success.

4. *Schedule family dinners.* Eat with your immediate family, extended family, and your church family. Eating together is one way to slow down and savor not only God's good gift of food but also the relationships we cultivate around the table. Chew slowly. Ask questions. Practice gratitude.

4

Beyond the Gated Community

SAFETY

To value one another is our greatest safety, and to
indulge in fear and contempt is our gravest error.

Marilynne Robinson, *The Givenness of Things*

IT WAS THE SUMMER we'd moved back to the suburbs. With rents high in Southern California and properties going quickly, we were lucky to find a home with three bedrooms to fit all six of us. The one we'd landed on was a split-level with one bedroom on the bottom floor, the living area on the second floor, and two additional bedrooms on the third (including the master bedroom). With its three levels, it had a touch of urban cool, and I liked it—until each night when I tried to fall asleep.

Just as my eyelids would get heavy, I'd be jolted awake. I'd heard something. I'd stare out my screened bedroom window on the top floor, and every creak and distant coyote call would leave a flood of adrenaline. *What was that? Was someone breaking in through our glass patio door two floors down? Were my children safe? Had we remembered to lock everything? Should we have paid for an alarm system since we were two floors above two of our children?* The neighborhood moms' Facebook group had blown up with long threads about recent break-ins. A wallet stolen, a computer gone, a mess left. I'd lie in bed, my mind racing, making a pros-and-cons list about whether I should get out of bed again. I knew my fears were likely unfounded, but they wouldn't subside until I triple-checked locks and laid my hands on my peacefully sleeping children.

How was it that we'd left our home on a busy street in a city to move to the suburbs, where safety was king, and only now I'd found myself paralyzed from fear? The rare walking paths I loved so much in my corner of suburbia, it turned out, could be more than a space to exercise: they were quick escape routes where a thief could disappear after jiggling door knobs.

After a month of spotty sleep and my eyes glued to Facebook threads where I'd figure out how close the break-ins were to the heads of my sleeping children, I'd become accustomed to panic and fear. I tried to pray, but still the fear of what could happen kept me awake. Fear became a habit. But as autumn approached, the promise of rest came too. They'd finally found the culprits: bored teenagers.

In a neighborhood that felt as planned as Disneyland, where a child's happiness was ensured at every turn—where we had the "good life"—teens turned to petty crime to keep things interesting. For these teenagers all of life was built to ensure their safety and fun, yet we, their community, hadn't required them to grow into roles of increasing responsibility. We'd said yes to their whims, we'd orchestrated every environment to keep them safe, and as their privilege had increased as they aged, their responsibility hadn't. They were left with time on their hands and no good use to put it toward. So they stole wallets and gave mothers of young children panic attacks each night.

Our collective obsession with safety, with giving our children the best, had left these children hungry for risk, for a thrill. The only way out from the pressure of this bubble-like enclosure was to break it, and the breaking left all of us less safe. It left us ruled by fear.

GATES, WALLS, AND SAFETY

We can't grow and flourish unless our basic needs are met, including safety. We must be safe and have shelter and food to thrive. I wouldn't be a good mother if I didn't long to create safe places for my children, if I didn't care about every bump in the night. Good parents desire to keep their children safe from real evil and nurture their wonder. These protective impulses can be shepherded to widen our care for others outside the family, to extend home in our communities and churches. But they can also mushroom into negative emotions such as fear and anxiety, where we self-protect, hover, and withdraw. We can't sleep even in suburban neighborhoods with low crime rates. We're worried. We imagine worst-case scenarios.

Safety is a good and right desire, but when we bend ourselves around safety, to be safe at all costs, we are motivated by fear. We're afraid that what we hold most dear will be taken away from us— whether that's our children, our reputation, our livelihood, or our privilege. It feels as though if we were to lose these things, we would cease to be ourselves. And if we're Christians, we doubt that if the worst happened that God is as good as he says he is, or even that God would still be enough. When our highest aim is to stay safe, we also lose out on meaningful relationships, noble sacrifice, and personal and communal growth.

In the suburbs our architecture reinforces our self-protective impulses. We live behind walls, fences, and closed garages. We often don't see the opportunity of our cul-de-sacs.

Architecture, city planning, and geography always tell stories. Our fixation with safety is built into our suburban architecture. Since the 1970s, gated communities for middle-class and upper-middle-class residents have mushroomed so that more than four million homes across America are behind gates. The earliest master-planned communities on Long Island "offered what suburban developers still advertise: 'the means of withdrawing from the labor and anxiety of commerce to the quiet of their own families.'" The gated community is simply the most obvious structure showing us suburban values: protection of one's private property, safety, and a homogeneous social group.

Our neighborhood geography with its curving streets (reminiscent of country lanes) and cul-de-sacs promotes a community that, in its best moments, is cohesive and neighborly when we are turned outward and away from self-sufficiency. But in its darker moments, our geography lends itself to a myopic view of human experience. Whether or not we live behind actual gates, we live turned in on ourselves, as if we are all that matters, where our daily rhythms reflect the rise and fall of our success or emotional temperatures.

By living a life bent around safety, we're easily lulled into a self-referential life. We fail to see beyond our front doors, beyond the successes of our children, or beyond those just like us. It's easy to close our eyes to poverty, physical and spiritual—not necessarily because we don't care but because we don't have eyes to see. We use our houses as fortresses. We keep a safe distance.

The stories our places tell are always moral. In what they value and how they're built, suburbs, cities, small towns, and rural communities incline our hearts both Godward and self-ward. Our suburban geography informs our loves.

For those of us in the suburbs, there are moral consequences to living behind gates or even in racially and economically narrow neighborhoods. It isn't that we shouldn't live where we do, but we must ask why we live where we do. We must ask specifically how where we live forms who and what we love.

> We must ask specifically how where we live forms who and what we love.

Then we must follow the way of Jesus even in the suburbs.

But gates are appealing. In *Suburban Nation* the authors write, "The problem with gated communities is not the gate itself, but what the gate encloses." Gates promise we get to stay in control. Behind gates, we can protect ourselves, our children, and our investments. We imagine that by enclosing ourselves behind gates, or fences, or even in a suburb with good schools, our community life will be enhanced. We'd be with like-minded people with similar backgrounds and socioeconomic brackets. Life would be comfortable. We wouldn't have to explain ourselves, our cultures, or our values.

Yet the story every war movie and adventure tells is that the "good life" isn't in building safe enclosures but in living for something beyond ourselves or our children's happiness. Bilbo and Frodo Baggins leave the Shire because there's a grander story to be part of than the safety and comfort the Shire offers.

We cannot flourish if we desire safety at all costs. Like the bored teenagers in my neighborhood, if we're not called to a greater degree of responsibility for one another in the public realm, we will be up to no good. When we have the means to do so but are not enveloped in a greater story, we will always elevate the private above the public good. It's not doing us or our children any favors.

BUBBLE CHILDREN AND HELICOPTER PARENTS

Several years ago in Utah the golden leaves were falling and winter was in the air. I bundled my two toddler boys into fleece hoodies and hats, and we headed to the park to burn off energy. We crunched fallen leaves; I gripped their hands tightly as we crossed the busy street, and we settled on the larger of two playgrounds—the one with the two-story slide and "big boy" equipment. Though little, they'd outgrown the smaller one.

Ezra, my eldest, headed for the slide, and I watched with amazement as my second son, Porter, began to climb up the green playground dome.

He hoisted his little muscular body up to the bars, curled his legs around another bar, and shimmied straight up to the top like a monkey. Other parents lunged forward watching this two-year-old nine feet up in the air, sitting like a king at the top. They instinctively moved to stop what seemed an inevitable fall. I stood under the dome, eyeing his movements, determining his balance.

FINDING HOLY IN THE SUBURBS

My little monkey became the talk of the playground. I was blasted with amazed questions: "How old is he?" "Does he always do that?" "Wow!" and, by other parents, I was told off for allowing my child to climb so high. Why didn't I rush in to keep him closer to the ground? As his mother, I knew Porter's capabilities, how he intuitively used his body, and how he was always chasing to keep up with his brother, just a year and a half older than him.

In the countless years of monitoring playground structures, tree-climbing, and even their scurrying to the top of the red balls in front of our suburban Target, I've let my four children climb, jump, and explore. When they want help, I'll give them a small boost, but we've kept to the rule that they need to climb appropriate heights. They need to be able to get down from what they climb up. I'm teaching them to know their limits and abilities, to take risks, and show them that I'm there if they need help. The goal is not to keep my children protected from every possible bump, bruise, and scraped knee.

It wasn't always this way. To learn this art of safety (that often looks a lot like letting go), it took a giant goose-egg on the forehead of my then one-year-old son Ezra. He couldn't wait to get to the playground structure. On his little legs he tottered around quickly; sometimes his feet wouldn't be able to quite keep up. He'd fall, pick himself up, and keep on running. On one of the laps around the playground, I could see him headed toward the metal stairs.

I lunged as I saw his feet begin to trip. It was too late. His forehead hit the edge of the stairs and he crumpled to the ground. I rushed to cradle him with kisses, rub his forehead, and watched with horror as a goose egg rose from the surface. I rushed home, Googled incessantly, and applied ice, children's Tylenol, and homeopathic remedies. Most of all, I felt guilty. I wasn't there. His goose egg was a visual reminder of my maternal failure.

Yet I knew I couldn't keep him little and safe forever. Even then, I was beginning to see this parenting journey as a gathering of the slow moments of letting go. When I realized that I couldn't protect my children from every potential danger, I could settle into my job of raising them well, giving them tools to grow and develop, and providing a haven of grace where failure was okay.

I don't want my children to live in a bubble where their mom always comes to the rescue, where they don't have the space to appropriately test their limits, or where they aren't given room to fail.

When we are so concerned about safety we often slide into becoming helicopter parents. Research shows this combination of overinvolvement, pressure to perform, and material advantage is making our kids increasingly depressed and anxious.

Our concern with safety is actually harming suburban children. Affluent kids (who usually live in the suburbs) are at highest risk for emotional and mental health issues. When we shape our lives around our own safety and the safety of our children, we, as "controlling and overinvolved parents typically leave kids feeling angry or alienated, neither of which is conducive to emotional closeness." This leads to between 30 and 40 percent of affluent children struggling with psychological problems, and 10 to 15 percent struggling with anorexia and suicide. Our affluent children—the children of the suburbs—are experiencing emotional and psychological problems significantly higher than the average child, and often even greater than children in dire poverty.

We cannot fashion our lives around keeping our children safe. Once our basic needs are met, being safe won't help us or our children grow; in fact, it's harmful. We cannot protect those we love from evil. We need a bigger story to be a part of so we needn't fixate on safety as an answer to feeling small, fearful, or out of control.

JESUS IS THE GATE

Humans are fearful, and when we have material advantages, it's easy to think it's our job to protect ourselves and our families in every possible way. But this is harming our children. What can we do as people of faith? We must rely on our good Shepherd to keep us ultimately safe. We find our belonging ultimately in another who is able to affect change. Rather than trusting in our actual gates—or all the ways that suburbs effectively bar us from other image bearers of God—we must increasingly see God as our good Shepherd. We must see Jesus as the gate.

In John 10, Jesus identifies himself as both the shepherd and the gate. He says: "I am the gate for the sheep. . . . I am the gate; whoever enters through me will be saved. They will come in and go out, and find pasture. The thief comes only to steal and kill and destroy; I have come that they may have life, and have it to the full" (John 10:7, 9-10 NIV). In that day, as shepherds led their sheep to green pastures, they'd also be looking for enclosure and safety. The shepherd would find a canyon, cave, or fenced space, and in the evening the shepherd would count his sheep. Since there was only one way out and in, the shepherd would guard the entrance so the sheep didn't stray. He'd lie down, making a gate with his body to ward off attacks from the outside. As the gate, he'd keep his sheep safe both from their own straying and from external threats.

> As suburban people, we must ask where our safety comes from.

When we think a change of location or circumstance will bring us joy and the life we desire, we delude ourselves. When we set up gates and walls to protect ourselves—whether it's a gated community, our 401(k), our emotional withdrawal, or even that we don't have friends different from us—we set up ourselves as the shepherd of our souls.

It's not that safety isn't important or shouldn't be maintained—after all, Jesus isn't doing away with the gate. But as suburban people, we must ask where our safety comes from.

Functionally, do we trust in our sound financial planning, our moral and successful children, or our safe suburb, more than we trust in Jesus, who promises abundant life? When we surround ourselves with suburban comforts and begin to trust in all the ways we can control ourselves, others, and our environment, we are ruled more by the fear of it all being taken away than by having "life to the full" Jesus offers.

This is the full life: life where we are deeply at peace because we have a loving Shepherd whose voice we hear and who guides us. We don't have to keep working harder to be loved, seen, and known. Our status, success, and investments do not have the final say on our worth as a human being—whether they accrue or fail. We are held in the great gaze of God, who looks at us with eyes of love, who puts himself in harm's way to make safe enclosure possible.

As we enter the gate through Jesus' perfect life, death, and resurrection, we can let go of busyness when we hunger to be important; we can let go of consumerism to fill our soul's empty spaces; we can let go of individualism as a way to be right and good; and we can know that no matter our circumstances we will be kept safe. As we enter through the gate, we follow a Savior who can keep us both eternally safe and who promises to meet "all [our] needs according to the riches of his glory in Christ Jesus" (Philippians 4:19 NIV).

We are shepherded by a God who promises to never leave us or forsake us, even when safety, like a rug, is pulled out from under our feet. It is the presence of our good Shepherd, who alone keeps us safe. We are never forgotten, never abandoned, never ignored, never worthless. We get to be children again.

So like children who know they are safe and loved, we're free to fail and we're invited to say, "I'm sorry." We're free to open gates.

OPEN THE GATES

All our own methods of obtaining safety still leave us fearful. We're anxious and depressed, and we're passing it down to our children. If our safety and peace aren't contingent on our own effort, material advantage, education, or wall building (literally or figuratively), we must seek a "peace which surpasses all understanding" (Philippians 4:7). King David, whose circumstances ranged from victory to death threats, writes in Psalm 4:8, "for you alone, O LORD, make me dwell in safety." Surely David experienced more peace than suburbanites, with all our material advantage.

If we're open to experiencing Jesus as our Shepherd, how do we live beyond the gated community? Even if we don't live behind actual gates, we realize how we wall off our hearts and don't seek out people on the margins. We're fearful of outside influences on our children. Trusting in Jesus as the one to keep us ultimately safe means we practice letting go of our white-knuckled grip on control.

We start by opening gates. In Jesus' parable of the wedding banquet, he asks us, like he asks the guests of the feast, to go into the streets and highways, and compel people to come in to his kingdom. He fills his house with outcasts—anyone who will come to the party (Luke 14:12-24). Our call is to go into the streets, not wall ourselves behind gates.

The kingdom of God isn't meant for those obsessed with safety; when we're proud and focused on ourselves, we'll never show up to the party of free grace in the first place. At the cross we're all beggars. We all get to come into that house.

To experience peace, we also let go of control. Shannan Martin writes in her book *Falling Free*, "sometimes surrender means letting go, and other times it means letting *in*." We need both movements of surrender. We surrender to the good Shepherd, knowing he will keep us eternally safe, and we swing wide those gates. After all, Jesus didn't say, "Come and follow me, and I'll keep you safe." Though he will keep us safe, our call is to go out and be bringers, "fishers of men." Safety is a byproduct of security. Only when we're secure in the love of God will we be hospitable people ready to spend our lives on others.

> Our call is to go into the streets, not wall ourselves behind gates.

As we practice welcoming others, God will show us the welcome we receive because of Jesus. The gospel says that our self-protective impulses are not the good life. When we follow Jesus, we grow in our desires for his kingdom, not in prioritizing our own safety.

Finally, living beyond the gated community looks like saying, "I'm sorry." When we're secure, we can move toward a posture of repentance; we can come out of hiding. We say "I'm sorry" to God and to each other for all the ways we've sought our own comfort, ease, and reputation rather than running toward people and welcoming them to a party none of us deserve.

In repentance we are released from the "'hyphenated' sins of the human spirit" (A. W. Tozer's phrase) such as self-righteousness, self-pity, and self-sufficiency. On the threshold of repentance we can own up to who we really are: fearful people trying to have it all together. Thankfully, we have a Shepherd who guards and directs his sheep to green pastures.

I don't want a gated heart. I don't want a suburb that is turned in on itself. I want to get to the end of this life spent for Jesus. Let's swing wide those gates.

COUNTERLITURGIES
to Prioritizing Safety ←

1. *Create a family mission statement.* Think through your own childhood and your instinctual attitude about safety. Evaluate how this might play out in your own family. Do you allow for growth and appropriate risk? Work on a mission statement for your family and evaluate where safety fits in it.

2. *Play.* Take a hike, play a game, dance in the kitchen, have a race—anything to recover a childlike sense of play. As we play, we practice resting in a God who provides sunshine, food, and a mind, body, and spirit. From here we can begin to cultivate gratitude.

3. *Practice noticing needs.* Start with your friends and family and pay attention to one need you can meet each day. Pray for your eyes to

be opened to the needs around you as you try to meet the needs of neighbors and strangers.

4. *Take up a one-week challenge.* Put your phone down during the evenings and practice screen-free, totally attentive moments of connection with your family or friends. Look for ways to unite and watch as conversations and connection grow. Begin to pray how God then might be calling you outside your family to connect deeply.

(5)

Where the Sidewalk Ends

REPENTANCE

> *Only the person who is completely safe can*
> *understand that judgment is good news.*
>
> FLEMING RUTLEDGE, "WHY DID JESUS CHOOSE THE CROSS?"

IT HAD BEEN A STRING OF DAYS with too much noise—children, politics, social media, and my own internal chaos—so I took to the neighborhood walking paths to work things out in my body while my husband constructed things out of wood (his own way of working things out). I could feel myself hit walls, get to breaking points, pass the point of no return—whatever cliché I could trot out to say "I need out." I'd neglected quiet. And it was almost too late.

There's a gift of bodily presence that I'm finally learning in my late thirties, when I'm past caring about men looking, the perfect abs at the gym, or how quickly I've bounced back after four babies. Maybe it's because I'm finally asking myself deep questions about what I'm hungry for and how to be whole.

My body can move, and movement is a glorious gift and privilege, no matter my dress size. So I unwrap it: my toes stretch out to dirt paths—the ones that feel a bit fake, winding their way through my master-planned community—but I'm anxious to get myself out into nature, no matter its shape. I walk quickly up the hill, my lungs feeling tight, and my mind blissfully quiet.

71

I watch. I listen. I pick a path through California scrub brush and paths already dusty brown even though it's spring. I force my mind away from past years in green Rocky Mountains glory and remind myself right where I am. In the suburbs. I remind myself we've been called here. This place matters too.

I chase the beauty even in the dusty brown broken-down spots. I look for meaning in the dirt. I need to believe with my body that God makes beautiful things out of the dust, that there's renewal. But *renewal* seems like such a soggy word today, the sort of word on jade-green spa leaflets, and I need something more than renewal. I need resurrection. Even if it's for a moment, I need a God who sees my insatiable hungers in suburban wilderness. I need meaning to make sense of the ordinary.

As I crest the hill, I strain for a faraway glance of the sea. But it is foggy and the chances of seeing a button-sized spot of blue are slim on the best of days, given our distance from the Pacific. So my suburban walking paths will have to do. Sometimes solitary walks are full of noticing, and other times, a podcast orients my thoughts. Today, it's the latter.

I'm listening to an interview with Frank Wilczek, a Nobel Prize-winning physicist, who is talking about physics, space, and mathematical equations, but he's using the language of beauty. This is a language I know. I'm hooked when he starts talking about asking beautiful questions. He says if there is a Creator (and he's not at all sure), then he is an artist. I stop and sit on the edge of some loose gravel. This isn't some tie-it-up-with-a-bow Christian rhetoric about God as Artist— this is a man who understands the operation of the universe in ways I can't fathom, who's says the universe is like cosmic Jell-O. He's making the complex accessible. He's chasing beauty too; and in some measure we can do it together—he in his science lab and I, a suburban mom, as I take to my neighborhood walking paths.

He gets at the heart of all my longings in one short sentence: "Having tasted beauty at the heart of the world, we hunger for more." I can't help but turn to the language of Scripture—to all the injunctions to "taste and see" that the Lord is good, to story after story of Jesus feeding people, feasting with sinners, turning water into wine. I keep thinking how glory is pictured as a wedding banquet when we will finally be one with Beauty. But here and now, we are hungry creatures. We are left with noise. We are left with so much gaping space between the *already* here of the kingdom of God and the *not yet* ache for its consummation.

So we fill up our hungers with suburban fast-food fixes. More stuff. More busy. More walls. We are scared of silence. Yet finding the space and time and energy to work through our hungers is hard and holy work.

Finding place is so much more complicated than I once thought. I'm learning that my internal journeys are inextricably linked with my external ones. I'm trusting that even a short walk in the middle of suburbia will show me more of God, more beauty, and how to be present here. I'm praying I'll find my place.

It's quiet, unseen work: this listening, this footfall on dirt paths, this lifeline of noticing. But like Wilczek's Jell-O, every little thing leaves a trail across the universe. Like a rock skipping across the lake, the ripples grow. My walk to clear my head might leave breadcrumbs behind me for another hungry soul to gather up.

As I trace these brown dirt paths again and again, I'm reminded that we all, as Rainer Marie Rilke wrote, are "grasped by what we cannot grasp." We are held by the gaze of the Artist. That is where we must always begin and always end: we are held. But it is not a masquerading, numbed version of ourselves that is held. It is the real one: with all the flaws, hurts, dreams, and fears. It's the you without all the bells and whistles suburbia says you must have to be seen, known, and loved. But how do we get there when we're so tangled up in the wrong hungers? This journey here in the suburbs always has to start in a raw place. It starts with repentance.

AN OLD WORD BRINGS US HOME

I bristle at repentance. It's a hefty word that we don't know what to do with in the suburbs. We say a quick "I'm sorry" and are met not with "I forgive you" but "it's okay." But sin is not okay. We can't brush it off. It has to go somewhere. Pain, hurt, disappointment, and failure go underground and twist into bitterness, envy, and pride. We're alienated from each other. This is not how we were made. We were made to be in deep communion with our neighbors, with God's people, with our places, and even with the God of the universe.

As I let Scripture reframe my understanding of God, I see he is a Father who provides since the beginning. I like to think of God stooping low, his knees in the dust, his fingertips running over the textures of creation. From there, he breathed into man and woman the breath of life and they became living creatures. As a community of perfection, God as Trinity had all that was needed. Creation of the cosmos and humankind was an outpouring of love itself, not a way to feel less alone. Like a proud father, God looks at his creation of men and women and proclaims, "They look like me!" We had a perfect home.

Until sin entered the world, creatures were at peace not only with God but also with each other and their places. Now, we find ourselves adrift like the prodigal, hungry to belong and filling up on whatever our places tell us is the thing to chase. Because of sin, we are exiled from not only our Creator but also our home.

When we turn our backs on our perfect home, we naturally seek to create it in other places. Such an impulse is imprinted in what it means to bear the image of God; like God, we too are homemakers. Yet we're quick to require that places satisfy our hunger to belong. Our places can only point to ultimate belonging, but can never fulfill it. Sin has worked its way into the ground.

Deep down we know we can't hope to earn enough, know enough, work hard enough, or ever be enough. Any happiness we buy is always short-lived. No matter where we live, our hearts, our homes, and our neighborhoods are tinged with sin—from neighborhood fighting to preferential laws—and no amazing plan could ever annihilate our alienation from the God of the universe when we keep choosing our own way.

How do we get back home? How do we retrain our hungers for the good, true, and beautiful? How do we repair all the broken connections between not only our neighbors but also all the broken systems of the world?

We return to that ancient word *repentance*. Repentance is God's good gift to bring us home.

When we are at the end of our rope, there is good news. We need an entire renovation, not just a new coat of paint. Repentance, rather than a quick paint touch-up, means seeing ourselves rightly. It's time to pause and stand exposed. That's where healing begins.

We cannot have relationships with others or God without vulnerably naming our failures not simply as personality quirks but as sin. We cannot expect reconciliation without owning up to the ways we have petted and preened the idols of suburban culture: safety, busyness, individualism, and consumerism.

> Repentance is God's good gift to bring us home.

The first call that ushered in the kingdom of God in Jesus was "Repent!" It is our call too—even here in the suburbs. To be whole people, to love fully, to belong, we must start by repenting.

What in your life do you need to repent of? Where have you unthinkingly bought the lie that God is not good, that you need something else, something more? Where have you privileged your own growth and success over love of neighbor? How have you numbed the pain or even the ordinary? Where does your walk toward repentance start?

A LONG WALK IN THE SAME DIRECTION

There is an arc to repentance and a movement: it is a long walk in the same direction, one that as Christ-followers we take again and again. Healing always begins at the place of hunger.

We must excavate whatever we've used to fill up our hungers in the suburbs. How have you used stuff to make yourself feel important? How have you filled up your calendar because you are afraid of the silence? How have you kept scrolling on your phone because it's easier than dealing with hurt? How have you pushed your children to achieve so you can fulfill your own longings for significance? How have you chased beauty and perfection because you thought no one would love you unless you were beautiful? How have you made excuses for your sins and not owned up to them?

We must name our hungers. There is goodness underneath our God-given desires. We want to work hard, do well, and have safe, healthy families. Our deep hungers cannot be satiated by increasing our busyness, consumption, or thirst for significance. When our hungers become the ends in themselves, our appetites rule us.

The essence of sin, Augustine reminds us, is disordered love. Our hungers are not bad, but how we choose to fill them. Repentance is the walk we take to reorder our loves. Small baby steps, one foot in front of the other, again and again.

△ ☁ ☼ ☁ △

The story that started this book is well known: the parable of the prodigal son. The younger boy left town with his entire fortune. He spent it and poverty forced him into dire, despicable circumstances— the sort of thing we avoid at all costs and pray never befalls our own children. But right there in the center of loss is a gift.

There, in his failure and feeding pigs, the younger son reorients his life. He belongs at home, with his father. All he sought that he thought would complete him—friends, love, sex, successful work, foreign travel—utterly failed him. But there in his failure, instead of resolving to work harder, be different, hide from his origins and finally "make it," the son woke up. He remembered himself. He was a son. He had a home.

Although he knew he wouldn't be able to take up the legal respon-sibilities and privileges of being an heir (he figured, since he'd squan-dered that), just being in his father's house as a worker would be a better existence. So he began the long walk home, rehearsing his speech: calling on his father, telling him that he'd sinned against heaven and earth, decency, and most of all against his father. He had a plan too: he wanted to be a hired servant.

The first step in repentance is awakening: when the younger son awoke to his hunger in the middle of the pigsty, repentance became a possibility. But it proceeded not through the flash of inspiration but in the long, slow, humiliating walk home.

Repentance began to bear fruit in the mundane, one-foot-in-front-of-the-other journey he took toward his father. The gift of the desert space was an awakening to his sonship. It is God's kindness, even in the barren lands, that leads us to repentance (Romans 2:4). It is God's generosity that he incites our hunger for home even at the bedrock of our need—even when we have walked clear away in the other direction.

When the younger son started his speech, the father surrounded him with the clothes of a son and the meal of celebration. I imagine that it was only then, at that glorious feast, that the son awoke most fully to his relationship with his father. Repentance then drove much deeper because it lost its perfunctory nature. It was a response to a safe, kind, and generous father who covered the son's shame.

But often we in the suburbs are more akin to the elder son, who stood outside the party, angry at the lavishness and special treatment given to his younger brother. When we're committed to earning our keep, grace and mercy are affronts.

When our hearts are hard, grace and mercy are barriers to belonging and tools of isolation.

> When we're committed to earning our keep, grace and mercy are affronts.

But forgiveness, the gracious response of the father, is not the flippant reaction of a doting old man. He does not wave a magic wand

and make it all go away. Forgiveness costs. Part of the elder son's anger at the acceptance of his younger brother is because rightfully all that was left to the estate was coming to the elder brother. Although the father was still in charge, the wealth of land and herds would one day be his. The celebration for the entire town was not only a gesture of forgiveness borne from a wellspring of the father's lavish, incomprehensible love, but also the result of the loss of the elder son's future financial security.

Repentance can only culminate in a party when it actually costs something. Forgiving others means we follow Jesus in bearing the cost in our bodies. When our failure, shame, loss, and sin have been eaten up, covered, and replaced with something far greater than we could have asked or imagined, that is the good life. It is far richer than simply getting what's coming to us, good or bad. But what does repentance look like for us in the suburbs?

TURNING AWAY, TURNING TOWARD

Repentance is good news. Finally we can stop pretending that we've got ourselves, others, and life all figured out. But what is repentance? To repent is to turn: it is both a turning from and a turning toward; that's why a suburban walk is such an appropriate image. It is a leaving from and a going to. We turn our backs on sin. We embrace the grace of God.

Repentance requires presence. We learn to root ourselves in our place. When we first moved home to the suburbs, I'd spend many mornings pushing my double stroller on concrete sidewalks or up dirt walking paths. My feet show me that I am part of this little spot of earth. It may not be bustling or majestic (at least at first glance), but it is mine. It is here where I am called, in this mess of suburbia with its quick pace, overachieving children, and beautiful people. And I am part of the beautiful and broken work of placemaking here.

So easily I'm quick to exchange my own hungers with the hungers of my culture: I reason that surely walking will keep me fit like all the other women who pursue image and health. I play the loop of shame and resolve to hike longer, harder, and more often.

But on the good days, walking reminds my body with each step that I am here, here, here. I am a whole person. It reminds me that the small, quiet habits I cultivate in my body can show me how to create small, quiet habits in my heart.

It opens my eyes to the world around me, to see people not as pawns but as image bearers of the God who runs to meet us. So, in those early years, while my older two children were at school, I often took my younger two children on walks. There, my anxiety slows. My breath quickens. I learn how to be present without screens or laundry. I learn that there is indeed an unfurling of a gift in regular liturgies—whether it's walking or repentance, or both at the same time. Both require change. Both are so unflashy as to be unnoticeable.

Walking has become one way my soul detoxes. We are bodies, minds, hearts, and souls. I choose to reorient my body to learn how to feel my soul again when it's become numb by stuff, self-focus, and an individualism that causes my desires to grow crooked. I need the small act of regular walks not only to help me connect to my place but also to have a bodily analog for repentance. I need my feet to show me home. I need to walk somewhere even when I don't feel like it, because quite simply, it shows me how small I am. In the suburbs especially, I need to intentionally practice this opening up, this noticing, this bodily seeing. I think of what went through the mind of the prodigal on his way home.

I pray for small moments to see rightly—to feel the prick when I've been chasing comfort and self-satisfaction; to open up physical space in my body and in my heart.

One particular morning, on our walk home, my children and I passed a labyrinth in the middle of the paved walkway. I understand what our suburban master planners were thinking, I suppose, by adding a grassy labyrinth in between the walking to create "interest." The labyrinth is usually a mess of mud and grass as bikes and runners travel from middle top to middle bottom, its circularity ignored for efficiency.

I heard a voice inside me, not sure whether it was God's or mine, but I stopped. We didn't, after all, have anywhere to go. Stopping, even for a moment, gets me out of my wheel ruts of self-sufficiency. I lifted my children out of our double stroller, and we walked the labyrinth together, they leading the way. It hit me, rather appropriately, as "a little child shall lead them." They laughed in their game of chase and I wondered what I'm leaving behind as I enter and start the slow prodding toward the center. "Have mercy on me, a sinner," I repeat. As I get closer to the center, I'm suddenly fearful—what if God is not there? What if God is silent? What if I cannot get any clarity; what if all there is, is one step endlessly in front of the other?

I reach the middle. There is no flash of inspiration. But I smile at the sunlight on my face, my children laughing and playing and thinking this is the best moment ever, these moments of presence they inhabit so easily. I turn to walk back out of the labyrinth. The circling the opposite way is entirely disorienting after having circled to the right; now, circling to the left makes me feel off-balance until I get into the rhythm of it.

Is this a bit of what repentance and sanctification look like, I wonder—those big words that can lose their meaning in their heaviness? Is repentance perhaps a repeatable recircling where, as I get to the center, I discover more—both more of my sin and a goodness that seems too good to be true?

These small, mundane movements of heart and body are the building blocks of how we learn what it means to find holy in the suburbs. We turn away; we turn toward. Eugene Peterson describes repentance as "always and everywhere the first word of the Christian life." We will not find home in our hungers, in ourselves (no matter how well and how deep we plumb), or in what we acquire. The gods of the suburbs will not satisfy.

Our journey must pivot on our turning; we can only be whole to the extent that we learn repentance. In a lovely turn of phrase, Peterson writes, "it [repentance] is a rejection that is also an acceptance, a leaving that develops into an arriving, a no to the world that is a yes to God." Repentance is the long walk home: a turning away from the life in the far-off country and a turning toward a father who scans the horizon for his son.

But of course it's not always that easy to uproot the sin in our hearts and lay it bare in front of others, let alone God. Nevertheless, we have a particular task as suburban Christians: we must dig down past all the fluff to find our souls. We must take away our pet projects and our politics that we think will change the world. We must refrain from endless accumulation and be brave to sit in the quiet, right in the center.

We must name our sin. We are judgmental. We are harsh. We measure success based on promotions and square footage. We line up our children's accomplishments as trophies telling us we're doing a good job. We consume things, people, and our land. We fail to be generous. We think only of our own peace and prosperity. We do not long for the kingdom of God.

The question as we grow into maturity is: Will we be brave enough to sit in the uncomfortable silence? Will we feel the pain of disconnection—that relationships and family and work are not the ends in themselves that we imagined? Or will we keep chasing soul clutter to push off our inevitable hunger, our shared human ache? Will we first "get fed up with the ways of the world [so we have] an appetite for grace"?

It is the uneasy and unsexy discipline of repentance that we must walk again and again. Repentance recalibrates our suburban desires. When we repent, we move from the lane of an individualized, consumerist life to the wide expanse of the kingdom of God.

When we repent, we move from the lane of an individualized, consumerist life to the wide expanse of the kingdom of God.

It's there we find peace amid a world that tells us that our work ethic and busyness are what proves our worthiness. We can breathe there.

As people of faith, we must ask for conviction, we must name our sin, we must turn (repent), and we must seek restitution and reconciliation. Finally, like the father in the parable of the prodigal son, repentance always ends in rejoicing. We get to throw a big ol' party.

FORGIVENESS: A DOOR HANGING OPEN

The long walk of repentance leads us to forgiveness; this is our homecoming. Repentance is the right response to sin, as we confess "what we have done and what we have left undone," yet having confessed, we are left waiting on the threshold as we await response. We are awaiting pardon; we await forgiveness and reconciliation. We want more than a shrug or "it's okay" in response; we wait for the good news. My children know this waiting.

We've taught our children a small way to keep their hearts soft and learn repentance. We practice repentance even when the noise, chaos, and sibling bickering bounce off stairwells. It becomes our day-by-day, minute-by-minute habit as at least one child an hour comes to me complaining about how they were socked in the mouth by an irate sibling.

We get on each other's level, we look each other in the eye, and the one who has done the socking says a few simple words: "I'm sorry for . . ." Not "I'm sorry that you . . ." or "I'm sorry, but . . ."; we must name our sin specifically. We own our brokenness in front of those we've offended. We then ask for forgiveness. Usually it follows a quick script—"I'm sorry for hitting you. Will you please forgive me?"—and the offended child offers it easily.

Other times it takes longer. We work through what's really behind the hurt and offense, and sometimes it takes a while for the other to be able to offer forgiveness. But in each instance, my children are learning habits of repentance at a pace that's appropriate for childhood. Sure it's rote. It lacks nuance. But I hope, like learning to brush their teeth, repentance will become a habit and forgiveness will be asked for and granted. And I, as their mother, am learning how free we feel when we repent as I learn from my little ones.

Repentance can free us, but as adults, we also know the feet-shifting waiting of the gap between repentance and forgiveness. Forgiveness is what we long for, but like so much of life we settle for a quick fix. We distance ourselves from awkward friendships. We offer half-hearted apologies and vow to do better next time, but without really repenting or granting forgiveness, we're left hanging in the balance. We are not restored. Excuses are easier to pile up than waiting in that in-between vulnerable space when we've laid it all on the line; there, we've put our real selves in the doorway and we wait, anxious, to see if we're accepted, forgiven, and beloved again.

In the parable of the prodigal, the father doesn't even let his son finish his repentance speech. The boy is so covered in forgiveness he needn't even detail his plan to pull himself up by his bootstraps and wear his sin like a blanket of shame that follows him wherever he goes. Instead, he is clothed with the robe, shoes, and ring of sonship. He is restored as the heir he has always been. He is wrapped up in a love that is too good to be true, but is.

Jesus told his followers that parable to show his listeners (and today, readers) that yes, you have a Father God like that. You have a God who runs to meet you, who bears the weight of your shame and sin in his own flesh on the cross. There, in a mysterious way, we're told that God took on sin, shame, systemic brokenness, and our suburban hiding. In exchange he gives us the perfect record of Jesus. We get to wear the robe of sonship; we receive the smile of the Father, no matter how we keep running back to shiny objects. We never cease being fully his.

But "God's reckless grace [that] is our greatest hope" comes at the price of self-sacrifice, first God's and then ours. We are not only in need of forgiveness ourselves from others and from God, but we also experience the pain and freedom from forgiving others.

Forgiveness is "the generous release of a genuine debt." It hurts to release your need to be heard, understood, or right. To forgive others means that we must bear the weight of pain in our own bodies; when we forgive, we fall on the grenade. We absorb pain rather than giving it. It means we unclench our fingers from retaliation, bitterness, and fear.

But we can forgive only because we've first been forgiven. We can bear the weight of someone's hurt only because we have a Father God who has borne all the weight of our sin when we come to him. We know that there is a cost to forgiveness: it's why we're astounded when the families of the victims of the 2015 Charleston church shooting offer forgiveness, or when a woman takes back her cheating husband. The cost of forgiveness seems too high. But that's when we start with us, when we are the center of every story.

> **Repentance and forgiveness can happen only when the beloved embraces us.**

We must learn to be forgiveness people. If repentance is learning how to walk into the reality of seeing ourselves rightly—created and good, besieged by sin, yet redeemed in Christ—then forgiving others happens when we put this right seeing into action. We must put this into our words and our bodies. We must live in that liminal space. Life is lived in these repeated threshold moments.

If we are not forgiveness people, then we nullify God's forgiveness to us. We are the ungrateful servant in Jesus' parable who is forgiven a crippling, life-altering debt and then later we effectively throw our neighbor into jail to repay a measly debt. When we are slow to forgive, it's often because we do not see ourselves in need of forgiveness in the first place.

We must start small. We pray, "Lord, help us see. Help us see how we stuff objects and people into holes only meant to be filled up by an infinite God. Help us take one small step on the long walk home." This small, daily, radical act of repentance and forgiveness could be the world changing we long for. Beyond our names in lights or the non-profit advocacy we dream up, what if our story, even in the suburbs, began and ends here? What if, to get out of the rat race and the success-drivenness of our culture, we learned to see anew? What if we said, "I'm sorry" first? What if we own up to not only who we are but also what it cost to bring us home? How could our neighborhoods, let alone our own hearts, be transformed?

You may have grown up on a diet of "world changing." Yet that was never our job. We're quick to forget the world has already been changed by God, who died for his beloved and rose again to conquer all that binds us. We don't start by aiming high to change the world—we start low, right where we are. We start on suburban walking paths. Repentance and forgiveness can happen only when the beloved embraces us.

As I walk, I'll learn how to pray, to notice more deeply. When the sidewalk ends, I'll find myself met by a Father who runs to meet me, who calls me his beloved. That's all that we're wanting, isn't it?

PRACTICES

of Repentance

1. *Journal.* Spend some time praying and writing down places where you sense God may be calling you to repent for the first time or in a deeper way.

2. *Walk.* Go on a neighborhood walk with no agenda other than noticing. Think about how repentance is like a walk.

3. *Pray.* Ask the Holy Spirit to illumine your own heart so you know what to ask forgiveness for and who from.

4. *Read historic prayers.* If you don't know where to start, read a prayer of confession in The Book of Common Prayer or look at the Prayer of Examen, where you go through your day thanking God, repenting, and asking for God's help.

6

You're Not a Barbie, You Belong

BELOVEDNESS

Being the Beloved constitutes the core truth of our existence.

Henri Nouwen, "Being the Beloved"

I WALKED INTO THE GYM for all the wrong reasons. To get fit fast, to tell people about our new church, to show my husband I was up for his crazy CrossFit scheme. I did it to prove I could be as strong as he was. There were black mats on the floor, chalk dust in spots, a pull-up gym that looked like playground equipment I didn't know how to play on, heavy weights stacked in the corner, and weighted balls. I couldn't hide behind an elliptical machine or in the back of a packed class. But I took a breath and pressed on.

For a woman who has never liked to run, the "warm-up" felt like more than I'd done in years. My mouth dropped open at the women doing pull-ups. They were Amazons sweating in their Lululemon luxury workout attire. Up and down, up and down, like moving your body that way was no big deal. In my Old Navy workout pants and old running shoes, I sweated and pulled on the rower. I grunted like a caveman lifting barbells—but by the end of a few months, I was stronger, leaner, and a little less winded.

I hesitantly asked one woman—one a little less like a machine— what she liked about the gym and told her I was new. In small classes of no more than twelve women, I'd already stood out as a newbie. Now living mere miles away from my high school, all the lunch-tray holding moments wondering who I'd eat with came flooding back. The woman was running slower that day because she'd just had chemo again. She ran and lifted to show herself she could, to stay active and able for her children at home. She encouraged me to keep at it, that as I kept showing up, things would shift. They did. My arms grew in strength, I slept better at night.

Though my body began to change, I couldn't seem to change the tape playing in my head. As I got stronger, it grew worse. It went something like this: "Look at her. How is she so fit after having three kids?" Then in a "choose your own adventure," "pick your story," my internal tape would shift one of three ways. The first was self-condemnation: "C'mon, Ashley, pick it up. You can work harder, be better, look better. You have to catch up! You've seen some physical gains, now put it into gear. You're not working hard enough." Or I'd excuse myself: "Well, I have had four kids, and that woman over there obviously is idolizing beauty, the gym, or her fitness level. (Not like me.) She's obsessed, I'm not, so it makes sense I'm not performing as well." Or withdrawal: "I just don't belong here. I'm not at their level. I slow down my partner on the workouts. I stick out like a sore thumb. I'm slow and squishy, and I don't have a wardrobe of Lululemon. I should either get it together or not come at all." Depending on my mood or circumstances, the tape in my head played songs of withdrawal, shame, or faux superiority.

I fought my body at every turn, willing it to speed up, work harder, perform better. Having recently moved back to the suburbs, I figured my body was the vehicle to help me find belonging in a culture that prized physical fitness and beauty. Globetrotting and advanced degrees wouldn't endear me to these gym beauties; so instead, I figured I'd join them. I'd be PhD Barbie because we were, after all, living in a material world.

If I didn't have the accolades that mattered to the suburbs, I'd work at them. I could get in shape, buy special anti-aging facial serums, get the right clothes, and eat the right foods from the latest diet. It worked for a while. My hips grew tighter, I found I had muscles in my back, and I had more energy when I cut down on the cookies. I even bought a pair of Lululemon shorts—I was becoming suburban Barbie.

But being suburban workout Barbie wasn't who I was created to be. This plastic version of reality always demanded more: more pull-ups, more clean eating, more gym time to not lose the muscle I'd gained; and always demanded less: less calories, less rest, less satisfaction in who I was right now in the present. After a few months, I realized I couldn't cut it. The gym would have to go, not because working out hard was bad but because I couldn't get out from under the weight of my internal check boxes. I did it all to be beloved by a culture that didn't care.

A gym body, a new diet, new workout clothes, a new house, or a new plan that would finally help me get organized and be a calm, gentle person will never let me rest. I need a better story. I need to get to beloved. I need belonging. I bet you do too.

WE NEED A BETTER STORY

We hunger for real beauty—not just a magazine version. Think about an experience of being struck how perfectly right a particular landscape is or how a poem or musical line makes sense of things. We desire something so aesthetically pleasurable, satiating, and enticing that we are both at home in its presence and pulled deeper into it. We call this beauty admiration, artistic appreciation, or even a plot point in a love story. We hunger for a beauty that enraptures us, fills our senses, and makes sense of us.

The suburban answer to our deep hunger for beauty is sold in gym memberships, dress sizes, protein powders, face creams, and face lifts as we pursue a plastic version of deep beauty. It is fueled by comparison:

there is always someone more beautiful, more attractive, younger, and on trend.

When I was in high school, a band came out with a song called "Barbie Girl." With its playful techno-pop and sense of nostalgia for the toys of our childhood, we got sucked in to singing in Barbie's voice. Being a Barbie girl meant wearing someone else's desires. If you had a Ken to belong to, your body, your accessories, your Barbie car, your Barbie dream house were willingly given over. The prize for a Barbie girl was the love of another plastic doll.

But when we feel loved only because of how we look, what we do, or what people say about us, we too are plastic. We only belong as long as we continue to stay young, strong, and beautiful. Beauty is one ticket we cash in to find belonging. A suburban plastic beauty is a flimsy substitute for belonging.

We live by a story of contingent belonging: to stay front and center, we must always work for love. Achieve more, buy more, be more—these are the siren calls of consumerism and individualism. We need a better story than the one suburbia peddles. We need more than belonging found only in what we do, where we work, and where and how we play. When we lose our jobs, when our families feel like they're falling apart, when we can't afford the pricey vacations, we need belonging that is not based on circumstances.

When we find a people and place to belong to, we can be ourselves. We long for a place to lay our heads, like tumbling into a well-made bed prepared just for us with a pillow to rest our weary minds, a blanket to cover our shame and failure, and a clean pair of sheets that show us we are not too dirty to be welcomed. We need the promise of rest—that someone else will watch over us.

God is that gentle parent who prepares a place for us. God—the one who is infinitely powerful, just, and merciful—looks at you like a starry-eyed parent fluffing pillows and washing sheets. You are his beloved. He smiles at you. Can you breathe that in?

Repentance and belonging go hand in hand. When we repent, we get back to beloved. Repentance opens the door for us, and forgiveness welcomes us in. Repentance is a twofold movement of turning away and turning toward. Living from our belovedness is taking up residence in a house that God made.

Learning belonging is also a double movement: there is a turning inward, knowing in our bones we're accepted and loved; and a turning outward, as we pay attention to and serve others. These inward and outward movements are the inhale and exhale of Christian faith. We are God's beloved. We turn in, we turn out: these movements bubble up from knowing and experiencing our own belovedness as God's children.

Yet how do we live out of that belovedness? How do we reach a deeper beauty than one that is bought and sold?

> Living from our belovedness is taking up residence in a house that God made.

How do we rest with all that needs doing? We can never get to belonging, deeper beauty, and rest through more activity, more striving, or more spiritual workouts through which we prove ourselves. We can only get to beloved when we immerse ourselves in a story that starts with the goodness of creation, where we then feel the weight of sin deep in our gut, where we rejoice in repentance and Jesus' sacrifice, and where we live out our belovedness (even in the suburbs) while looking forward to a home that will answer all our deepest longings.

⌂☁☀☁⌂

Let this story capture our imaginations. Way back in Genesis the ancients tell us that we had a perfect home, a perfect place where we fit, where we were fully and intimately known. A garden without decay or pesticides or death. Can you imagine the colors of that garden? The lush plants and fruits and the sense of perfect community, belonging without self-consciousness, without shame? We're told we lived in harmony with God, our world, and each other.

Then we began to doubt that home was the best place, we sinned, and we thought we knew better. So we've lived as exiles ever since, always itching to get back to a place of self-forgetful belonging. It's why we stay busy. It's why we look for belonging at the gym and Target. In the Old Testament we see cycles of enslavement, where slaves cry out to God and he delivers them. We see God bringing freedom and releasing his people from bondage and bringing them into a Promised Land. We see them exiled and weeping for their lost inheritance and then, prophecy upon prophecy about a Messiah who will bring heaven to earth, where they will finally be home.

When Jesus shows up on the scene, it's different than we imagine. His home is a backwoods Galilee, not the centralized kingly city of Jerusalem. Jesus exists on the margins geographically and hears, sees, and even touches those on the margins. He receives as an act of worship the anointing of perfume and hair erotically spilled on his feet. He calls a ragtag band of blue-collar workers and starts a revolution. He holds and sees—really sees—children; he touches lepers and makes the lame walk.

The kingdom that he talks about is radically different than we think. He dies and gloriously rises to make that kingdom a reality. He shows up in the in-between places, always on the road somewhere—to Damascus, to Emmaus—and the church is born. He sends the Comforter to speak into our hearts, to dwell with us, and to ignite us with tongues of fire so that mercy, truth, and justice will roll down like mountain streams.

This story lights up my imagination. It's a story I can't quite shake, even in the dailyness of making peanut butter and jelly sandwiches. It's a story that makes those sandwiches mean more than simply providing lunch for my children: it means that even peanut butter and jelly sandwiches are part of the making of God's kingdom, as small offerings. Because in his kingdom, we're all adopted into a family of misfits and refugees; we're all given new robes and rings on our fingers. We are all beautiful. We are welcomed home into the embrace of a

Father who is always for us, who calls us beloved. Doesn't that seem just too wonderful to grasp?

Mike Wilkerson writes, "The whole of God's story can be understood in terms of his presence." Isn't that all we long for—not just the niceties of a pretty religious story, but the presence of a God who is both powerful and also good? Don't we all long for someone to be empathetically present, not standing behind our back waiting to see if we get it right this time, or silently disapproving of our sin patterns? Don't we long to breathe in the truth that when we repent, God removes our sin as far as the east is from the west (Psalm 103:12)? That we are not forgotten—that God has "engraved [us] on the palms of [his] hands," and like a mother hen, has wrapped us under his wings where we take refuge, covering us (Isaiah 49:16; Psalm 91:4)? Isn't this the love and belonging we all crave?

WE NEED A BETTER LOVER

Before Jesus started his public ministry, he showed up on a dusty day outside of Galilee at the edge of the Jordan River. There, his cousin John was baptizing people under the banner of repentance. John looked up: suddenly his heart leaped in that strangely wonderful way it had leaped in the womb when Jesus' mother had announced to his own mother that her womb housed the Son of God.

He knew there in the water too. As Jesus came near, getting into the water to be baptized, the flip-flop of his insides increased. John wasn't seeing this moment as history-making; the baptizer was struck with his own need to be baptized. He held out repentance to others, but he needed it too. With his scratchy camel-hair clothes, his disheveled hair wet with water, John said, "I need to be baptized by you. Why are you coming to me?" (Matthew 3). This Jesus didn't need to repent. He didn't need to be baptized.

With that sure way of talking, Jesus replied he needed to be baptized; it was fitting: "Let it be so now, for thus it is fitting for us to fulfill all righteousness." John took the man, his cousin, the Son of God, and held him around his waist and brought the water over him. With the water dripping over them both, the heavens rolled back like a scroll and the Spirit of God came down like a dove and alighted on Jesus. A voice came from heaven, "This is my beloved son, in whom I am well pleased" (Luke 3; Mark 1; John 1).

Before Jesus did anything to earn the Father's love, he was called beloved. Before he followed all the rules, loved others, or healed people, he was beloved. Before he took on the sin of the world or even taught and lived righteously in front of the public, he was beloved. As a new mother adoringly gazes at her new baby in her arms—marveling at little fingers and toes—so God the Father looks with complete approval, complete love, at Jesus. Tish Harrison Warren writes, "Jesus is eternally beloved by the Father. His every activity unfurls from his identity as the Beloved. He loved others, healed others, preached, taught, rebuked, and redeemed not in order to gain the Father's approval, but out of his rooted certainty in the Father's love." Jesus' ministry, his death, and resurrection are the ways he lived out his belovedness.

The crazy thing is that as we are united to Christ, we too get to bask in that smile of the Father. We too get to love others not to gain approval or to work harder, but because we are already loved. Did you catch that? You can stop the worry and busyness, the shame and hiding. Belovedness doesn't come from working harder to be more acceptable or more beautiful. You cannot belong based on what you have, what you do, or what others say about you. In the suburbs, it is countercultural to live in light of this deep-rooted belovedness because everything around us says we need a constant stream of *more* to belong. This, friends, is a lie. Wrapped in Christ, we have everything. We are held in an eternal embrace. This is the true story we must learn to inhabit.

But there are barriers, of course. Being beloved of God is not the pseudo belonging we settle for: in trying to get to beloved we often take a flying leap over the wall of sin. We excuse it. We root its cause in someone else's sin. We use grace to excuse the pursuit of truth, which points the finger back at us. Or we pursue our own rightness to the extent that we forget grace entirely. Grace without the sting of sin and subsequent repentance is not good news. Conversely, sin and repentance without grace is not gospel: it is condemnation. When we settle for one without the other, we (not God) have become the arbiters of truth. We have decided that we are the storytellers, not an antiquated God. Yet only God perfectly holds truth and grace in a glorious tango, both wrapped up together, moving as one.

But here's where grace is shocking: it covers who and what we actually are, and points us in the way of something better. God's grace in Jesus redeems us from all our sin, shame, hiding, and fear. Take this example: when Jesus spoke to a woman caught in adultery, a woman who'd used her beauty as a poor substitute for belonging, he scattered the religious leaders ready to pounce with a single comment: "Let him who is without sin among you be the first to throw a stone at her" (John 8:7).

They left because they knew their own hearts. In our twenty-first-century world, we'd like the narrative to end there: "See?" we say. "Everyone is messed up and broken. Those religious hypocrites! Jesus is a god of love." Love does not leave us where it finds us. But there's more. When Jesus speaks to the woman, it's true, he does not condemn her. But he also tells her to leave her life of sin, to "sin no more" (John 8:11). He calls her to repentance, not to shamefully state her crimes but to offer a beauty that enfolds her sins and offers redemption even still (John 8:1-11).

It's a pattern we see in John's Gospel. When Jesus meets the woman from Samaria, an ideological enemy to the Jews, Jesus exposes her sin to offer her something better. He says: "You are right, . . . you have had five husbands, and the one you now have is not your husband," and then he also woos her with living water and calls her to worship (John 4:17-18). Her response is to tell everyone about Jesus, "the man who told me all I ever did" (John 4:29). That is where love is found—in a deep wellspring of belonging that acknowledges the worst of us, covers us, and calls us to leave those comfortable sins behind.

> That is where love is found—in a deep wellspring of belonging that acknowledges the worst of us, covers us, and calls us to leave those comfortable sins behind.

We cannot persist in our sin, whitewash it with a brush of "cheap grace," and go on our merry way. Being beloved is so much richer.

Like the Samaritan woman, we still look for other lovers to satisfy, whether it's actual lovers or tamer sins of greed, consumerism, self-promotion, and disdain for the poor. All our suburban sins hold out a plastic beauty we keep buying. We are entangled in sin. In the moment, we imagine the next purchase, the next promotion, the next accolade of our children, or our next breakthrough at work will bring a permeating sense of peace (what the Bible calls *shalom*).

Yet I would not be guiding my children into maturity if I permitted them to eat only candy, watch TV all day, and be unkind to their siblings just because they felt like it. No, the good and loving call is to empathize with their cravings, but not to excuse or indulge them. There are only two calls to us as Christ-followers: repent and believe. Because our journeys toward an ultimate home are fraught with misdirected longings, we easily settle for lesser lovers. Instead of repenting, we excuse. Instead of believing, we hedge our bets.

Henri Nouwen said that just like things, "People are limited and I want them to be unlimited lovers." We heap on others and on our places a weight they were never meant to carry. Spouses, children, friends, and suburban tract homes with granite countertops will never give us a peace that passes understanding. Whatever we accumulate to chase deep-seated belonging will fail us in the end. Our things will never walk through pain with us. Even our most intimate relationships will not be able to entirely bridge the gap of empathy, understanding, and forgiveness, and give us unfettered, eternal belonging. There is no Prince Charming, no perfect child, no colleague, no bosom friend who will fulfill all our crevices of belonging. And there is no house, home, suburb, city, or countryside that will finally offer us all that being God's beloved can.

We need a better lover. Even in moments of pause, we must retell this good story because it is true: the story Jesus tells about what God is like is the story of the Father anxiously waiting for his boy to come home. At the other end of the son's long walk of repentance is a father scanning the horizon, not to pour shame into fresh wounds but to wrap his arms around his beloved. Yes, you need to repent. But you do so with a God who is good. You are that son. You are beloved. You belong. You are covered in the embrace of the Father. He "surrounds us like a house." We have a true home in him. And all our longings, what Pascal called "the infinite abyss," will only find their fulfillment in "an infinite and immutable object, that is to say, only by God Himself."

THE POWER OF A NEW AFFECTION

It takes me a while, but I do love to try the latest thing: skinny jeans, top knots, fancy coffee pour-overs, wearing workout gear for real clothes—when I'm in, I'll jump all over it and tell everyone about it. And it's not just me. It's the human way: we're excited by the latest claim on our affections. But we jump in with both feet and then find ourselves unchanged. This is why gyms profit every January—we make our resolutions, but we're absent from the elliptical come March. Somehow we think that more knowledge or a new habit will give us the belonging we crave. It never does. Love alone enfolds us into a better story. What we need is to be seized by the power of a new affection.

In a famous sermon of the eighteenth-century, Scottish pastor Thomas Chalmers says, "the only way to dispossess [the heart] of an old affection, is by the expulsive power of a new one." When we see our deep-seated sin and feel shame, guilt, or fear, we cannot use these same negative emotions to drive out our originating shame. Rather, only a new love has the power to take a spade to the roots of sin, cut them out, and then replace our weedy heart with a flourishing plant. We don't need more rules: we need a bigger, stronger love to propel us forward.

Take, for instance, Saint Augustine, famous for his conversion and subsequent first-person *Confessions* of AD 397. He writes of "rush[ing] heedlessly amongst the lovely things [God] hast made" in a misguided

> We don't need more rules: we need a bigger, stronger love to propel us forward.

effort to seek God. But his conversion is a fall into a "Beauty so ancient and so new." When God gets ahold of us, it is a grander story, a far better love. We are moved by beauty personified, not by what we should have done.

Augustine writes: "Thou didst call and cry aloud, and didst force open my deafness. Thou didst gleam and shine, and didst chase away my blindness. Thou didst breathe fragrant odors and I drew in my breath; and now I pant for thee. I tasted, and now I hunger and thirst. Thou didst touch me, and I burned for thy peace." It is God's tantalizing beauty and his relentless pursuit of Augustine that changes him. Augustine is wooed by a greater love. Only a relationship with the Perfect Lover can drown out the static with which we fill up our suburban coffers.

Chalmers closes his sermon with an analogy of a man looking from the comforts of home, family, and abundance into a desolate space. When we see the comforts of our pet sins and are asked to renounce them, we are not motivated to repent. We need more than a slap on the wrist to "stop doing that." Chalmers comments that of course the man, seeing only renunciation, would choose to stay with that which is closest and provides material and relational comfort. Repentance looks desolate.

But, Chalmers notes, if a "happy island" passed by that held out images of greater benevolence, peace, and abundance than what was close at hand, then the person would be sure to run for the island, especially if "signals of welcome" were visible. He's welcomed and wanted there. Living beloved of God is that beatific island. That is what Jesus, who is our ultimate home, looks like. Belovedness is not the desolately open space of "sin no more," but rather the "beauty so ancient and so new" of which Augustine wrote. We fall into belonging because it is beautiful. Belovedness is filled with more peace, more security, more adventure, and more contentment than our imitative comforts offer close at hand.

How do we get to that happy, beatific island—to this belovedness arising from a new affection? We want a to-do list to cross out all the steps on the way to beloved. But God is not a to-do list; God is not a master-planned community, with each part of himself nicely and neatly contained in a box. He is good, but he is not tame.

Lean in: it must start small. Getting to beloved does not usually start with a shining conversion moment giving your entire life a spiritual jolt of adrenaline. Beloved doesn't mean moving to Africa to preach the gospel. Those things of course may happen, but the harder task may be to wake up in your suburban home and find a contentment deep in your bones that has nothing to do with your bank account, your body, your children, your career, or your future. So we work at priming the soil for love to grow. The work of being beloved is a constant returning to the story of creation, sin, redemption, and glorification. It is in remembering and embodying the story together in our local churches. It is in starting daily liturgies that draw us in to a beauty that overwhelms and is even present through pain.

I want to pause as you may wonder, *Where does real pain fit?* The suburbs never anesthetize us from pain. When you're in pain, when your marriage is ending, you lose your job, when you get a diagnosis, when there's not enough to pay the bills—it's easy to think this journey toward belonging is a bunch of sunshine and rainbows. How can God be a better lover when you lose the love you had? How can God write a better story when yours is in the pit of despair?

Here is hope: we do not have a God who judges from far off; instead, he took on our complicated flesh, dwelt in the muck of relationships, was misunderstood, reviled, his reputation was eradicated, and he was beaten, betrayed, and killed. He was a "man of sorrows" (Isaiah 53:3). He understands your grief, loss, and mistreatment because he went through it himself. As we walk this line of detaching ourselves from the shiny objects we pursue for belonging and run to the man of sorrows, we will find contentment. There alone is belonging, no matter your circumstances. The good life is only in the suburbs to the extent that you, in the suburbs, are *in* God. God is our Promised Land, our ultimate home. He is our guide and horizon, even in pain and darkness.

It is to this home that we must cling, both in our small patterns of behavior and in our pain. We must take up small practices or liturgies that help us practice being the beloved. Once, during an argument, when I was tempted to listen only to prepare my words to fight back, I forced myself to stare at the ceiling. When words of condemnation came at me, I repeated in my head, *I am God's beloved. I'm beloved. I'm beloved. I'm beloved.* It didn't change the fight, but it did allow me to not use the disagreement as an excuse to be mean-spirited. I didn't wallow in all that was said of me. I could actually look all the bad in the face and begin to own up to the ways it was true, because I knew it didn't define me.

Getting to beloved may be as simple as repeating the phrase "I am my beloved's / and his desire is for me" when you slow down in traffic for a red light (Song of Songs 7:10). It may be sitting for ten seconds after your alarm goes off and remembering Jesus smiles at you. No one will write a bestselling memoir about such ordinary practices, but they grow in resonance and texture as you repeat them. These daily acts of repentance and leaning into our belovedness may in fact change the world as your own heart opens to God.

Think of the freedom and peace we'd have when we stop living by our rush and hurry, by our muscle-to-fat ratio, thinking they help us earn our keep, help us be seen. We don't need to look over our shoulders wondering if we measure up. We don't need to lose fifteen pounds to be loved. We don't need to bemoan our wrinkles or that our bank accounts aren't as secure as we'd have hoped. We don't need to micromanage our children so we are important. We do not need to measure our significance by Facebook likes. We do not need to use our spouses, children, friends, neighbors, colleagues, or church to find belonging. These are just pictures (imperfect at best) of what belonging looks like. They are the comforts close at hand.

Imagine with me what rest, wonder, joy, and meaning might feel like. What would it look like to be beloved? There is a place, like that beatific island, like a freshly made bed, like the embrace of a father at the end of the long walk home, where all our desires will be fulfilled. It's home where we can finally exhale and stop hiding. It's glory. And it's available in little appetite-whetting morsels now through very ordinary means of grace. Breathe. We are God's beloved.

But it doesn't stop there. When we learn to dwell in the belonging Jesus offers, it doesn't end in a cuddle between Jesus and us. We're propelled outward to share about what it feels like to really breathe. Belovedness always moves us outward.

What if finding holy in the suburbs meant we did something both entirely ordinary and incredibly radical? What if we loosened our grip on our resources and our people so that we could walk hand-in-hand extending the belovedness of Jesus? Can we change the story of the suburbs to be less about encircling our resources and more about moving outward toward others in hospitality? Let's find out what being beloved tastes like.

PRACTICE

being Beloved

1. *Waking ritual.* When you wake in the morning, instead of reaching for your phone or your to-do list, breathe in and out. Smile. Repeat "I am God's beloved."

2. *Read.* Read one of the Gospels and watch how Jesus' actions and with whom he associated flowed from his core identity of being beloved of God. Take notes. Ask yourself questions about how you live out of your primary identities (colleague, businessperson, mother/father, spouse, neighbor, etc.).

3. *Spark your imagination.* Read books, look at art, read poetry, listen to good music, and notice nature as the handiwork of the Artist. As we see all of life and the artistic and cultural products as pointing back to God, our loves and imaginations are formed. This is the slow work of growing into a greater love and a better story.

4. *Repent and pray.* Pray to experience a greater sense of God's belovedness. Pray that as you grow in your sense of belovedness, God would put specific people in your path to extend that belonging to. Pray, "I want to experience your beauty no matter my circumstances."

7

This Isn't Pinterest-Worthy Entertaining

HOSPITALITY

We're tourist Christians.
We remain as long as we're entertained.

A. J. SWOBODA, *A GLORIOUS DARK*

WE WORE OUR WOOL COATS in the middle of a Southern California summer, waved goodbye to our mothers, and boarded a plane for Scotland a year after we said our "I dos." We touched down in northern Scotland a day later, bleary-eyed and discombobulated, watching a foreign countryside fly past on the wrong side of the road.

When we made it south to Edinburgh a fortnight later, we were struck that we didn't know what BFR stood for—the ending to our first address as expat postgraduate students in Britain. BFR, it turns out, was the Basement Flat Right. And when we'd creaked open that peeling paint of the blue main door on Rossie Place and walked down the stairs, we realized why our rent was so cheap. We'd imagined all sorts of exotic sounding appellations for BFR with no idea that it meant a basement flat with one tiny window to let in the light.

We didn't know enough to be sorely disappointed. We hadn't yet puffed ourselves up with multiple children and proper jobs to feel we were entitled to a better habitation. It was sufficient. It was what we could afford. We could walk the several miles to the university and back. We could make it work. There was enough love and tea to go around. And plenty of books.

That was the flat with spongy wallpaper, a textured sort of wall covering that would leave the mark of your finger's indentation when pressed. We'd covered it in a neutral cream paint hoping to erase some of its garishness. We had to duck under the water tank to make it to the too-small toilet. Our bedroom was small enough that my new husband slept against the cold wall in our double bed and we both trudged along the small path between the other wall and the red carpet. Day after day.

Plopped into a different country, into a world of postgraduate studies where our American dollar didn't stretch far and everything from our clothes to our voices showed we were foreigners, we kept our heads down and did what we came for. We studied. We made friends, we were a part of a church—but these were ancillary to our primary purpose. That first autumn we traded a life for books.

We left Rossie Place early with scarves wound tightly around our necks and umbrellas over our heads, our thoughts to ourselves, and our lives on a mission that curved from university to work to home. There were moments, of course, when my thoughts and visions strayed—to what I was reading, to the way the waning light hit the hills, to how Edinburgh Castle stood sentinel over a city steeped in history, to how all the philosophers I read about walked in this same northwesterly wind as I did. How we were all kin.

But on the whole, my husband and I were there for advanced degrees, for knowledge, for all that scholarships and living overseas provided two young expats. So when my husband's sister-in-law asked about what fun we'd had, we looked confused.

The cinderblock walls were chilled. The move to northern climes meant the world grew dark during mid-afternoon teatime. After that first semester, with our minds enriched but our bodies and souls frail and flailing, we vowed a different life. We'd had no fun. We needed this too-small, too-cold place to turn into a home.

That's when we painted those spongy walls. We'd burn candles over good conversation. We'd buy cheap wine and whisky, and invite new Scottish friends over for a homemade meal even if their knees bumped against ours under the table. All it took was an open door and a willingness to be present and offer what little we had. We practiced cooking in a kitchen where each limb could touch a cabinet, fridge, sink, washer (yes, in the kitchen), or oven. We burned tapers down. We laughed. We feasted on leftovers from the French cafe I worked in. We tried our hand at cooking Indian curries. We shared our half bottles of wine, and cupped mugs of milky Scottish Blend tea in chilled fingertips.

When we moved out of that first flat two years later, our Canadian friends commented they hadn't imagined we'd stay that long in that little basement flat—the one with textured wallpaper and the dank mustiness and darkness of a basement. It was true, it was cramped and cold; it felt inadequate, especially in light of the new flat we were moving into courtesy of my husband's seminary, with a view high above a cobblestone street. In cramped quarters we learned not only to be a married couple but also how hospitality blossoms like the gospel.

We had nothing to give each other or new friends that could bridge the distance of cultural difference. Yet when we place what little we have on a small table with our knees bumping and give it as a gift, it grows. The place itself was no longer the center. In hindsight the spongy wallpaper became dear, not because of its quaintness that we reimagine as a romantic artifact, but because it was ours. It was ugly and small. Just the same, it's offered as a gift of welcome. It beckons: come and see, come and see.

> In cramped quarters we learned not only to be a married couple but also how hospitality blossoms like the gospel.

FINDING HOLY IN THE SUBURBS

THE CROSS AS HOSPITALITY

We know of the cross of Christ as the site where believers are forgiven, as a gruesome site of torture or execution. But I invite you to see the cross also as a space of hospitality. It's a home we're being welcomed into, given something to eat, and invited to share that with others. The cross is welcome with skin on. On the cross Jesus is both host and meal, both offerer and offering. What can we gain from understanding the cross as a site of hospitality?

The cross is small. So too is hospitality. Yes, the cross is the means by which God reconciles people to himself, a plan that changes the cosmos and fundamentally alters how humankind interacts with their Creator. Yet the cross is first particular, specific: as a historical event it repudiates our pristine abstractions and theological terminology. It takes place on a barren hill called Golgotha, "the place of the skull." It is the death of just one man.

On the cross the Savior of the world is sandwiched between two other men, their bodies equally hung in humiliation. This is the death of a man born into a small town. This was never how or where salvation was supposed to show up: the setting isn't even in a town, but outside the city limits. Salvation comes not through a triumphal entry but in thorns and nails, in blood and water. We imagine salvation (and hospitality) arriving in pomp and circumstance and social influence, not shared through common means and common people. Yet like most offerings (the widow's mite, a young boy's loaves and fishes), when small and specific offerings are given, they are first broken and then miraculously they are multiplied. God's economy is not ours.

The cross also shows us that hospitality happens through the mundane and sometimes painful act of staying present. It is bodily. Crucifixion is a tortuous exercise in staying present through death. Although we try to pile up niceties about the cross, we cannot get past the "fleshly actuality" of it. Stakes are pounded into Jesus' wrists and feet. He has been beaten and bruised, and thorns were thrust into his tender skull. Jesus dies slowly, hanging in humiliation for all to see. He pushes up against the nail holding his feet to the wood to get air into his lungs until he suffocates and his lungs collapse with the cry that breaks the barrier between God and humankind forever: "It is finished!" His body is broken. His blood is poured out. He is a burnt offering. On the cross he takes our sin, shame, and death, and carries it to the grave, so that when God looks at us, he sees Jesus' perfect record. He sees the face of his Son. We must hold together the effects of our salvation with the actuality of crucifixion: for all our theological terminology, justification occurs through the broken flesh of one man. Hospitality too happens through average people with ordinary elements.

Jesus always meets us with himself. In a mystery we cannot fully comprehend, he is both offerer and offering. Jesus is the offering. He is the meal. He is the bread and body broken and given. Before he was betrayed, Jesus broke bread in the upper room, the words worn now from so much hearing: "This is my body, which is given for you. . . . This is my blood . . . poured out for many for the forgiveness of sins" (Luke 22:19; Matthew 26:28). Every week, or every month, we not only take the bread and the wine as a nice little gesture in our churches, but because we know that this is the very means of grace.

This little bit of food portends that faith in Jesus is bigger than the sum of its parts, that something seemingly small—like Jesus' own humble roots or our own particular lives in particular suburbs—can effect drastic change. The purpose is not to change the world or even focus on being present to change those lives under our nose. No, finding holy in the suburbs means we first taste and see that the Lord is good. We eat. We celebrate. This is the meal of the beloved.

Jesus on the cross shows us that hospitality is in the act of noticing, of really seeing others. Even while his body bore the pain of humiliation, our sin, and the very real pain of torture, he notices his mother and John. There, lying prostrate at the foot of the cross, is his mother, the girl-child grown woman who has nursed the Son of God, pondered the gifts of the magi, and seen him preach, teach, and turn water into wine at her request. At the cross, though, she is buried in the pain of worship, of thinking how this life had gone horribly wrong and off plan. His execution is her end.

Yet Jesus gives her a new beginning. Her son, the Son of God, looks with pity at the homelessness in her eyes and in the eyes of "the disciple whom he loved," and gives them to each other in the adoption that the gospel can accomplish: "Woman, behold, your son!" and "Behold, your mother!" (John 19:26-27). In the midst of his own pain, Jesus sees the pain of others. He not only bears our sins but also sees the effects of pain and loneliness, and seeks to meet them with himself. As he'd seen the leper, the prostitute, the curious rule follower, on the cross he also sees and heals. There, in that mysterious space of pain, hospitality and healing flow when Jesus sees and meets people with himself. He is both host—welcoming and connecting people—and our offering, on which we feast with glad hearts.

Last, the cross shows us that hospitality is best given from vulnerability. The cross is neither pristine nor pretty, but like the rubbed-off hair of the Velveteen Rabbit, it too is real. Hospitality best starts when we move from our own vulnerability, not a top-down model of benevolence to ease our lazy consciences.

At the cross, Jesus is host: he welcomes those who enter in to the most intimate of spaces, his own body. He invites us to see the spectacle of death, but to also eat it, to know in our bodies that unless he is in us, there is no real life in us (John 6:53). Like a king and host, he prepares a table in the wilderness. Like a priest, he offers the pure, unspotted lamb on behalf of the people of God for forgiveness of sins and restitution with God. Like a host, he rains down provision in the desert, nearness when we are lonely, welcome when we do not deserve it. But he is also *the* offering, the food the host offers to undeserving guests.

The cross begins a revolution, rumbling through the known world. Jesus' disciples and apostles, when they spoke of the crucifixion, weren't simply talking about the manner by which God "saves us from our sins" or lets us into heaven. As N. T. Wright says, "they were talking about something bigger, something more dangerous, something altogether more explosive." Yet revolution, in politics or faith, always starts small. It always begins when you dig into your place and embrace the actual stuff of earth with all its specificity and brokenness.

THE CHALLENGE OF SUBURBAN HOSPITALITY

If we see the cross as the site of hospitality—where Christ is both host and offering—what does this mean for us in the suburbs? How do we start small, stay present, and learn how to notice well? And is that even enough in the suburbs?

There are obvious roadblocks to suburban hospitality. We pin decorating ideas on Pinterest and imagine the perfect party, but the demands on our time mean we hardly invite people in. Yet if we also pay attention to the radical nature of biblical hospitality—to do justice, love mercy, protect the fatherless and the widow—our hospitality in the suburbs never feels good enough. We do nothing and rack up suburban guilt, or we run ourselves ragged, rounding up donations for the homeless. After all our do-gooderism, we wave politely to our neighbor as we shut our garage door, exhausted.

The Bible clearly calls believers to practice a hospitality that reaches past barriers of race, class, ethnicity, and economics. In Christine Pohl's book on hospitality, *Making Room*, she surveys ancient versions of hospitality, and records how it was the spiritual practice that grew the church and abolished status markers. Yet, she writes, "As Christians became more established in positions of influence and wealth, their marginal status was diminished and their hospitality was more likely to reflect and reinforce social distinctions than to undermine them."

As Christians grew in power, the sort of hospitality offered was something you'd find on Pinterest—pretty flowers, pretty food, pretty and clean lives offered to someone who looked exactly like you. The gospel call isn't to Pinterest-worthy entertaining. The gospel call to hospitality is to reacquaint ourselves with those on the margins.

In a world of social media entertaining it's easy to be overwhelmed with historic Christian hospitality, how the early church kept "all things in common" (Acts 2:44), preached the gospel fearlessly, and opened their homes and wallets to provide for the needs of the church. If we live in relative ease and comfort, what do we do? Should we move to a commune? Most often we don't know how to start, so we do nothing. We engage neither our neighbors nor the marginalized.

But then I wonder: Is this welcome here in the suburbs not enough? Am I not following God's call well enough when I cook dinner for my next-door neighbor? Does hospitality always go down—from a place of privilege to the outskirts of town? Is that what hospitality is? Or, even, does hospitality always look like living among the poor?

It is wrong to assume that because your next-door neighbor might not need your hand-me-downs that they're not needy. The call to clothe the naked and provide for the fatherless and the widow is clear in Scripture. But as suburban Christians it's easy to think we're following gospel hospitality when we drive far away and offer our cast-offs in grand acts of benevolence. Meanwhile we don't engage the poor or homeless as equals, and we neglect to provide hospitality to our suburban neighbors. The poor need not be just recipients of our bagged lunches, but also to be among us, in our fellowship. Hospitable welcome is for both our middle-class suburban neighbor and those who have no one to speak up for them. The gospel call of hospitality is always to go out and find the weary, broken, and needy (of whatever level of privilege) and welcome them to a feast of belovedness.

We must loosen our grip on our homes, our safety, our time, and our lives, through intentional acts of hospitality. As Sarah Arthur and

Erin Wasinger learned in their year of deliberately taking up spiritual practices in the suburbs: "the crisis in hospitality always comes with that

> The gospel call of hospitality is always to go out and find the weary, broken, and needy (of whatever level of privilege) and welcome them to a feast of belovedness.

word 'my.'" When we hoard God's gifts, we are not hospitable. Just like the prodigal son, we have been given so much: the love of a father who runs to meet us, his forgiveness, and the feast of the Father because his child has come home. How good would a party be without fellow prodigals there to celebrate the Father's goodness? When we open up our time, our wallets, our homes, and our churches to the needy, we're inviting all to that feast.

STAYING PUT AND STARTING SMALL

The call of hospitality is for every neighborhood. We are called to move toward the rich and powerful *and* the poor and needy. We are called to offer our bodies, to see and to notice, and to move toward others in welcome. God may be calling you to move from your picket fence to advocate for the voiceless, to find friendship and solidarity by life lived alongside the poor. These are not better or worse callings. As the suburbs grow increasingly diverse, we will likely find our suburbs looking more like cities.

No matter the demographic makeup of our neighborhoods, God invites us to stay put. Staying put is not based on permanence: it is a call of presence. We can't withdraw into "gated-thought-enclaves" of sameness. In an article called "The Virtue of Staying Put," Gerald Schlabach writes that, instead, "what *is* countercultural in the United States [and much of the world] is attempting to stay in relationship with people who don't share our views." No matter where we live, staying put means staying rooted in place and extending ourselves to others in acts of service and presence, even when there's tension and disagreement.

I am called right now to stay here, to put down roots in a place that to me feels unadventurous because it's where I grew up. I wonder if the radical life-altering story of the gospel can permeate miles of tract homes and strip malls, if it can grow on highways. As humans we think that if only our circumstances changed, we'd capture an elusive contentment. We imagine other places will satisfy, that a particular place will be where we learn to be hospitable.

You can spread a table in the wilderness right in the middle of your cul-de-sac. Your subdivision can become a place where Jesus shows up, not because you have it all together or you finally mastered pairing that wine with an impeccable meal. Whatever your neighborhood, it can know Jesus because you are his hands and feet—whether that's because you share your takeout, a cup of coffee, you feed your neighbor's dog, or you volunteer in underresourced schools. We do our small things with love: we walk our children to school, we watch their flag ceremonies, we develop relationships with the owners of the locally owned cafe, we have heaps of people over for dinner. These are the rhythms of hospitality where we practice sustained attention. At its root, hospitality is the art of seeing other people as glorious bearers of God's image no matter your ZIP code.

> At its root, hospitality is the art of seeing other people as glorious bearers of God's image no matter your ZIP code.

There is no place that Jesus loves more because it contains a particular population demographic—rich or poor. You are not more holy if you're working in full-time vocational ministry. You are not more holy if you have much or little. God doesn't love you more because you have a big house or small one. Material wealth is never equated with blessing. You are the hands of feet of Jesus right where you are; yes, even in your subdivision.

Today I'm inviting you to practice the art of staying put and starting small wherever you are. This is the call of gospel hospitality. In our small Scottish flat with the spongy wallpaper, our friends didn't care that we bumped knees. In our home in Salt Lake City, the college students didn't care about small children bouncing off the walls; they were happy to be in a crazy, chaotic home. In the Southern California suburbs, my home isn't professionally decorated or large by comparison to many in my neighborhood. Yet no one is judging my furniture when they come into a place fashioned to hold and welcome them. When we open up our lives and homes to others, we respond to Jesus' invitation of welcome by offering ourselves and our time as "living sacrifices"—as offerings of faithful presence.

Starting small is how we practice a ministry of presence. We show up. Showing up always means that you are digging your hands into someone else's shared brokenness. Hospitality is messy, but it's real. It's practical and intentional. We take our calendar out and map out the neighborhood. We save several calendar squares a month just to have people in our home—no catch, no rote gospel presentation, no agenda except to see them and to love them.

Sometimes hospitably staying present leads us right into the heart of pain. Let's not fool ourselves in thinking that the suburbs allow us to hide or stuff our sin, or that any one place is somehow exempt from systemic sin. A picket fence and granite countertops do not push off pain and suffering. We suffer. We hurt. We are confused and bored. We are full of angst, shame, and loneliness. We don't need to change the world or our subdivision, we need only start small. See one person. Be present.

Here's what hospitality looks like on the ground: showing hospitality has meant less pretty meals and pretty flowers, and more late-night conversations in our living room with crumbs on the floor and drinks in our hands. It's meant begging for God to show up and come near with our hands outstretched to the ceiling. It's sitting with others and asking God to heal, convict, and bring redemption right through hopelessness. Hospitality has meant late texts to fellow churchgoers to help bring bags of groceries. It's meant conversations in Starbucks, where I'm blindsided with all the ways I inadvertently hurt another person. Hospitality has meant meetings and prayer groups while children climbed on me, had a meltdown, and there was sticky stuff under the table. Hospitality has meant selling a worn-out file cabinet, stained and tired from disuse, and finding a friend on the other end because we took the time to notice.

Showing up and seeing another person has meant awkward closeness huddled over an iPhone, listening to a person's favorite rendition of John 1 in Scots. Hospitality has meant dressing up and dining out, and it's meant curled legs in sweats on my wingback chairs. It's meant faltering conversations over pretty desserts and slightly awkward conversations that never got into a groove. It's meant my own flush of remorse and "I'm sorry" around a friend's fire pit. It's meant cramming too many people into too small of a room and calling this family. It's meant takeout and home-cooked meals and meals that flopped. It's meant providing free babysitting for neighbors and friends. Hospitality grows in all the little countless acts of presence. But it only flourishes when we schedule it, when we make it a point to welcome people regularly.

Life is so much fuller when we live for other people. Will we see? Let your heart melt for your neighbors who are so busy that they easily neglect the fundamental questions of human existence. Then invite them in. Serve an easy meal. Ask questions. Keep your schedule open. Pray for opportunities, and when they're presented, walk in them. Hospitality is our embodied worship.

Hospitality is our embodied worship. The gospel calls us to big, but it also always calls us to small. Who is right in front of you that needs to be seen? Where can you offer yourself in welcome to them? Where can you live out a broken and given life for your actual neighbors? It starts by staying put and starting small. And it always overflows abundantly and generously.

PRACTICES

of Hospitality ←

1. *Schedule it.* We make time for what we love. Commit to trying to have one person in your home at least once a week—dinner, dessert, after-school snack time, or drinks. Let this time be a gift for others. Pray as you chop vegetables, whip cream, or make popcorn.

2. *Start at home.* Commit to eating together as a family five days a week to start. Start your hospitality project around your own dining table.

3. *Make margin.* Tithe your time. Allow free evenings where you stroll around your neighborhood, pray, and try to be a good neighbor. Find needs. Ask how you can help meet those needs.

4. *Reach out.* Let your neighbors know when you need help too. Ask for help. Receiving help means we believe practically that we need a community (neighborhoods and churches) in order to thrive.

5. *Move with the seasons.* Try a Friday summer movie night, a yearly holiday party, or a neighborhood Easter egg hunt that create rhythms of neighborliness throughout the year.

6. *Ask for a soft heart.* Pray for a soft heart that God would lead you into ordinary and radical hospitality with your neighbors, and that he'd give you a vision about how to extend this hospitality to those who are not like you.

8

Open Hearts and Open Hands

GENEROSITY

Jesus reminds us that the wounds of scarcity can be healed only by faith in God's promise of abundance.

WALTER BRUEGGEMANN, "ENOUGH IS ENOUGH"

I WAS CHARACTERISTICALLY FIVE MINUTES LATE, trying to squeeze in another errand before the next school pick-up. We had dallied too long at Costco, my daughter, Harriet, and I, and now were late to pick up her brother from preschool. But our bellies were hungry, and we couldn't pass up the $1.50 hot dog deal.

For once I was dressed in real clothes (instead of workout gear) and cute booties, so I stood tapping my heels while waiting for the several people in front of me to move. Harriet spun and danced in the little yellow painted lines as we waited. I squatted down to tell her she needed to stay by me. It was cold for California, but I noticed, when I bent down, the man's cracked heels in his sandals at the front of the line. The lines moved up the backs of his yellowed heels like fissures. *Gross,* I thought. I turned away.

I told Harriet we only had two more minutes we could wait or we'd be horribly late to pick up her brother. In her two-year-old fashion, high tears and high drama were quick to follow. I worked at quieting her, telling her we could manage a drive-through later, but we'd have to go. The sandaled man heard her cries, saw my inconvenience, and turned and asked if we just wanted one hot dog. He'd get it for me so we could leave.

"Wow, thank you," I said, floored by such an act of generosity. I offered him my two dollars, but he refused. "No problem," he said, smiled, and quickly passed back the hot dog. I tried to run to the ketchup station in my cute booties, dragging Harriet along while balancing the foil-wrapped hot dog, looking like a suburban parody in skinny jeans with a perfectly messy top knot.

While I was judging the man's cracked heels, he was listening to my daughter's tears, not to scowl at a toddler meltdown but to see and respond generously. In those five minutes I was seen by a stranger, while I had refused to see his own common humanity.

I didn't earn that hot dog. I didn't pay for it. I didn't even deserve to be served ahead of the waiting line who were better than I was with time management. My motives were messed up. But when I received an unearned and unexpected gift, even a $2 hot dog, it reoriented my day. Instead of dwelling in the land of anxiety, I was thankful.

WE ONLY THINK WE'RE GENEROUS

We have a hard time receiving in the suburbs. We're more likely to turn down the hot dog with a polite "thank you" or nod than express gratitude or look for who might need one. When asked to dinner, we show up at a neighbor's home with arms full of bouquets, wine, and dessert. This is more than a hostess gift: we can't seem to receive the gift of a good meal without bringing something to contribute. But no bouquet, no bottle of wine, no $2 hot dog, really makes up for our desperate need for community and connection. Our inability to receive—but to always work harder to earn favor—isn't just a suburban oddity. It points to hard hearts, unmoved by grace. Affluence, safety, and comfort can dull our souls.

In the suburbs we are materially rich yet spiritually poor. Simply by living in the suburbs we have a degree of affluence, access, and wealth by global standards. Even if it feels like you're just making ends meet, you and I are the rich ones that Jesus says find it hard to enter God's kingdom.

The Bible has scathing words about wealth that wraps itself around our hearts: how it's harder for a rich person to enter the kingdom of heaven than a camel to go through an eye of a needle (Mark 10:25), that our hearts are inclined to show the rich partiality, that we cannot serve both God and money (Matthew 6:24). Jesus called our suburban bluff when he asked pointedly: "What does it profit a man to gain the whole world and forfeit his soul?" (Mark 8:36).

Conversely, the poor are called "blessed" and inheritors of the kingdom (Luke 6:20), and God "upholds the cause of the needy" (Psalm 140:12 NIV). This is not because wealth is inherently wrong and God wants us to be poor, but because the poor know their need and cast themselves on the mercy of God. The rich set themselves up as little gods.

Riches shape our hearts' orientation. Craig L. Blomberg writes in his excellent book *Neither Poverty Nor Riches*, "The rich are not necessarily wicked, but frequently surplus goods have led people to imagine that their material resources can secure their futures so that they ignore God, from whom alone comes any true security." We functionally trust in our wealth, not Jesus, to save us.

We also think of ourselves as generous, but our generosity is exaggerated. While those on the lowest end of the socioeconomic spectrum give 3.2 percent of their income, the wealthiest only give 1.3 percent. In an article for the *Atlantic*, Ken Stern concludes, "It seems that insulation from people in need may dampen the charitable impulse." As we stay out of the lives of the poor and needy—because we first don't see ourselves as poor and needy—our compassion dries up. Our success actually makes us less generous, not more.

We're like my daughter who, on a recent Saturday, bemoaned sharing one of the last two Ritz crackers with a friend. She tried to parcel out half a cracker because she couldn't bear to part with more, but the two girls were left instead with a pile of crumbs from grabby fingers. When we're reluctant to give away our resources, we find less, not more.

Our generosity also tends to be superficial. Even though statistically we don't give as much as we think, many of us still volunteer, donate our clothes, and find charities to support. But like a younger generation who is becoming increasingly concerned with issues of justice, mercy, and compassion, we might do more good, but generosity does not affect our actual day-to-day lives. Our generosity stays comfortable. We give away our excess and we continue to live by our own schedules and values. If hospitality looks like welcoming the stranger and not just entertaining our friends, then the call to generosity must also be more than donating our cast-offs to Goodwill.

We will learn to be generous, openhanded people only when we learn how to be receivers. To be truly generous, we have to first learn how to be grace receivers.

RECEIVING THE KINGDOM

Our decreased generosity isn't about poor planning or staying unaware of needs around us; it's because we have stingy hearts. We live from scarcity. When we operate from scarcity, we hunger for any of our perceived unfilled needs. When these hungers are met, we imagine that we'll finally have the abundant life.

But when we try to meet our suburban hungers with our own effort and skill, while still wanting to live as faithful followers of Christ, we serve two masters. Dallas Willard wrote in *The Divine Conspiracy*: "It is not uncommon for people to think that they can treasure this world *and* the invisible kingdom as well, that they can serve both. . . . We simply cannot have two *ultimate* goals or points of reference for our actions." We'll take our house, our talent, and our well-paying job with a side of Jesus—provided he works within our schedule.

But our inner lives are stunted. We don't care for the poor. We repay every offer of help and every cup of sugar borrowed. When we grasp tightly onto our own self-sufficiency, we turn our backs on the rich, generous, openhanded life.

> We'll take our house, our talent, and our well-paying job with a side of Jesus—provided he works within our schedule.

We cannot be generous people until we first learn to be joyful receivers. So we must learn again how to receive God's kingdom like a little child—or even like a judgmental mom at Costco put in her place by the gracious offer of a free hot dog. We must see who we are and what food God gives to status-hungry people.

Who are we? We are not the benefactors and philanthropists. We are the needy. It's a lesson I learned one Sunday in August years ago.

I was hugely pregnant with my first child in the late summer heat of Southern California. My feet were swollen and I'd spend most afternoons after work trying to get my large body cool by lying on the kitchen tile. It seemed our apartment air conditioning was older than the building itself as all the window units did was shoot warm air around our apartment. But, on a new pastor's salary, we didn't have the money to replace the units. I tried to make the best of it: I spent free time in air-conditioned movie theaters or prenatal aqua aerobics classes.

One Sunday morning, our friends, a middle-aged couple named Tom and Jeannette, came to us with eyes crinkling in joy. Their joy was pervasive; though they lived with the shadow of Jeannette's disability, still their eyes lit up with a contagious contentment. I remembered a few years earlier how Tom joyfully pushed Jeannette in a wheelchair up a cobblestone street so they could experience Scottish history together. When love is our motivator, sacrifice is joy.

But this morning, they took our breath away. They clasped our hands in theirs, held out a check, and told us a story.

When Tom and Jeannette were newly married, an older couple loved them so well that they gave them a large sum of money. But there was one condition to this gift. They were asked to pay it forward. Tom and Jeannette must choose one

> **When love is our motivator, sacrifice is joy.**

family who they would bless in the same way. Out of all their years of loving each other and God's church, of being a presence of faithful belief in people's lives, their eyes set on us. We were that couple. I nearly dissolved into tears. Our friends had made a promise they held close for decades, and now we were the amazed recipients, both to the promise and the gift.

There was no response appropriate other than grateful tears, prolific thank yous, and a promise to be generous too. We were the undeserved recipients of a gift and a promise made long ago. We couldn't repay them, and to try to do so would've cheapened their generosity. Holding that check in our hands, I knew God cares about our bodily needs—our hungers, our thirsts, and even if we're cool in the last weeks of pregnancy. We must receive God's kingdom similarly, with open hands, with tears in our eyes, and a desire not to earn the Giver's favor but as a response to all that we've been given.

God doesn't just give us air conditioning, he gives us himself. He is the only food that will sate our hungers. Many of us have read John 3:16, the verse on poster boards at sporting events and on the back of cars: "For God so loved the world that he gave his one and only Son, that whoever believes in him shall not perish but have eternal life" (NIV). But before we get to the end of the verse, let's pause at the first few words: "God so loved that he gave . . ." God's love bubbles up and over-flows. This outpouring of love is generosity: "he gave."

God does more than meet our physical needs; he gives us Jesus to rescue our souls and give our lives rich purpose. He gives us a Savior who knows what it means to hunger, thirst, and be tempted. He gives us a Savior who had to cook, clean, and do good work. He gives us a

Savior who knew the Scriptures, grew in wisdom, and was holy, kind, compassionate, and truthful. Finally, he gives us a Savior who would deny his very life to bring us into the wonder, awe, and mystery and majesty of union with God. He gives us a Savior who would show us that suffering and death are never the end, and that God would never leave us or forsake us. God is a lavish giver.

When we try to repay lavish gifts, we offend generous givers. To self-made people, grace is an affront.

Grace is an affront because it goes against the grain of who we are supposed to be: self-sufficient, profitable, and nice people. We start here: we recognize we are needy. We've been given the greatest gift imaginable. The gift of Jesus perfectly provides for us, shows us we are seen, known, and loved, and calls us to more than a self-referential life. All we can do is say thank you and move into our suburban lives offering little morsels of that same generous gift.

> To self-made people, grace is an affront.

LEARNING TO LIVE OPENHEARTEDLY

When I begin to feel choked by anxiety and the panic rises in my throat, I either transform into Mr. Hyde-crazy mom, or I work it out in my body. So, I rolled out my yoga mat during nap time, expecting to at least burn off some anxiety and ideally burn off some calories too. The focus of my video practice was on opening the heart, so I followed along, rolling up to standing position and squeezing my shoulder blades together. Standing tall, chest expanded, I'd reach to the sky and then bend forward at the waist into a forward fold. I moved into a low lunge and looped my shoulders back, like the video instructor said. It hurt. I'd been so turned inward, hunched over my laptop or making lunches, that even though opening my chest hurt, it also felt like I could finally breathe. My lungs were freed to really open and take in life-giving air. Before, I'd just been constricted and hadn't even known it.

It ached to open up my chest, what the yoga instructor called the "heart space," yet this new posture was also where my body was made to be. When my shoulders were properly aligned, I could stand up straight. I could move forward in the world, not turned inward, but turned outward. I could breathe.

Made in God's image, we're more than just souls saved for heaven. We are mind, spirit, and body too. God speaks through our bodies. As I practiced opening up my heart, I worked *out* my anxiety, and more importantly I worked *in* faith. I considered: How had my own heart been closed off to others while I fretted over work deadlines? How had I stayed turned inward? Where was I stingy, lacking generosity, and honestly scared what would happen if I was poured out for others? Did I believe God could open my heart? Could I afford to be generous? I knew that living into a daily practice of generosity would ache and be painful (like my shoulder blades), but I also knew that when my spirit was aligned with God's, I'd finally be able to breathe.

An openhearted life remains rooted in Jesus and moves from a posture of gratitude. This is simply the openhearted posture we inhabit as we go about our days when we see ourselves as the unbelievably, gloriously loved and redeemed children of God. We embody the shape of generosity in our particular way and in our particular contexts.

A life of generosity is the natural overflow of a repentant and grateful heart. As our lives are increasingly shaped by generosity, we offer hope to a culture bent on meeting its needs with more things. We give things away. We value people. We sacrifice for others. We look to meet needs. We bring others along. This is how we live with open hearts in the suburbs. Our generosity will be our on-the-ground way people will be attracted to Jesus in the suburbs.

Everything else around us tells us you must live your best life now, follow your heart, amply provide for yourself

> Our generosity will be our on-the-ground way people will be attracted to Jesus in the suburbs.

and your children, and keep working harder. It's exhausting leading self-referential lives where we circle the suburbs in our minivans or feel beholden to a neighbor who lends us something. We're always keeping score. But when we give, we do away with the scoreboard. We welcome people in because all the markers of division are done away with in Christ. We stand together as beggars, grace receivers, and the bearers of the divine image.

As beggars saved by a Father who delights in us, we practice, inch by inch, how to pour ourselves out in generosity. If the suburbs hold out consumerism and busyness as solutions to our hungers, the gospel paradoxically states the opposite: in losing our life, we find it (Matthew 10:39). When our lives are hid in Christ's, we move outward. Enfolded in the deep love of God, we can begin to live an openhearted life.

Only when we're captivated by the gift of Jesus will we live generously. When we begin to use our money and time for the poor, the orphan, the foster child, the immigrant, and even our neighbor, we get asked why. It's not just because we're nice people. We give in response to the generous God who's already given us all things. So we can risk living openheartedly, meeting needs with open hands. We needn't grab and hold fast to our resources. We follow a God of abundance who invites us into habits where we provide for others. We can risk because we're not going to fall—not really.

CULTIVATING GENEROUS HABITS

Growing up, I thought I always needed an emotional faith experience to propel me into greater holiness. But what if I don't feel anything? Do we wait around until God strikes us with generosity?

We become generous two ways: first, our desires are changed and we are moved to love God and love our neighbor in practical ways. We tithe, we open our homes, we live in solidarity with the poor. Second, we start habits to help grow our desires toward generosity. When we don't have a burning desire to extend ourselves through our money or time, we start by developing liturgies to reform our desires. Habits form the backbone of an openhearted life in the suburbs. Let's consider five values that make their way into practical generous habits.

1. *We value people over things.* When we value people over things, we practice saying no so we can say better yeses. We take a hard look at how we spend our money and our time and ask what we really need. It's countercultural to choose to not put something you want on a credit card or to say no to the newest gadget every kid is begging for. But we never find the kingdom of God in stuff.

It's radical to choose to put your money where you say your treasure is—in Christ and his church. This means we ask God to continually pry our hands off our things. For our family, we tithe, we support a child through Compassion International, and we save money purposely to give away to needs that come up. It means we create blank space in our calendar and find people to invite over for dinner. It means we make our lives slower so we're open to chance encounters and gospel conversations. These commitments form the backbone of how we value people more than products. This is how we work to build God's kingdom more than building our own.

2. *We build up the image of God in all people.* Tim Keller writes, "If God's character includes a zeal for justice that leads him to have the tenderest love and closest involvement with the socially weak, then what should God's people be like? They must be people who are likewise passionately concerned for the weak and vulnerable." The church must spend its money and time (corporately and individually) on the least of these: those who don't have the same support system or safety net as the affluent.

The suburban church must not only act counterculturally to suburban values in how we say no, but also who we say yes to. We must be people who say yes to those invisible in middle-class suburbia: the working poor, the marginalized, multiple families sharing one home, those who are illegal, or recovering or stigmatized for past sins. This means that someone who looks different from you or comes from a different class or culture has a rich heritage that is worthy of dignity and respect. We move toward them—maybe awkwardly or timidly, but still seeking to learn, knowing we're all beggars at the cross.

Rather than climbing the status ladder, we choose to make practical decisions for the good of the vulnerable, poor, and disenfranchised. How do we do this? By how we vote, where we live, where we spend our money, and who we seek to befriend. This means we have to spend unstructured time looking for ways to meet people who we might not naturally run into.

3. *We stay in our lanes.* When we see needs all around us, it's easy to feel guilty and confused about what to do. We wonder: shouldn't I be delivering meals or handing out food to the homeless? Where can I volunteer in my local school or find an after-school tutoring program? Remember that God has gifted you uniquely and that your generosity, and the generosity of your local church, can have its own particular flavor. We aren't individually responsible for solving systemic problems.

Working together as a body, we'll find some members who are large givers, some who are great at rallying people around a need, others who are gifted on-the-ground responders. We need everyone. God has made us members in one body, and we get to accomplish his generous care and provision together. We're also a part of the worldwide church across time and space that God is glorifying himself through. The burden of everything never rests on our shoulders.

So we stay in our lanes. We seek to pray and do our own significant yet small part as individuals, families, neighborhoods, and churches.

4. *We embrace sacrifice as the good life.* Because God made himself known most significantly in flesh and blood, we know that he also intends us to not just send good vibes into the universe but to practically work in our bodies for the flourishing of all people. If we won't change our habits so that we have available time and resources, how do we think God will provide for the poor and needy among us?

But to do so requires sacrifice. My husband is fond of saying that the good life is always found on the other side of the cross. We live into a cross-centered life when we make sacrifices in our time and budget.

We commit to habits that enforce what we know: death is not the end, resurrection is coming, and Jesus is enough. If my present happiness, safety, and material success are not the keys to life, then it's easy to give these things up in service to a larger goal.

Only when generosity becomes a way to live out the gospel will we change our budgets so we can we show up with groceries at someone's house after they've lost their job. Only when we believe there are abundant resources in Christ will we go on a Target shopping spree for a new foster mom. Only when we see all children as our own in some measure can we organize donations for children who need school supplies.

It starts with making space—not just in our homes but in our budgets and calendars to bless others with our ordinary and regular acts of making room.

5. We look for needs and bring others along. When we find a favorite shop or restaurant, we can't help but tell people. When we've experienced the steadfast love of a Father who runs toward us and embraces us, we tell others. When we discover how freeing it is to not feel the pressure to perform to be loved, we welcome others into the abundant life of generous faith. There, no matter our socioeconomic status or retirement plan, we have all that we need. We ultimately belong to a far-off country where there will be no more sorrow, death, or pain. So as we live toward that eternal life even now in the suburbs, we invite others.

This looks like bringing a friend to walk and pray with you for your neighborhood. This looks like being a bridge for someone who's new in the faith or someone who might not be as naturally motivated or compassionate. Invite someone with you to a protest, as you help at the courthouse or a classroom, as you serve food, or donate your knitted goods. In community, we commit to discussing our calendars, financial commitments, and the good we've received as we've blessed others. We invite others to the openhearted life.

Generosity always disarms. When people aren't considered as projects, but instead we're generously living alongside each other, our generosity always cuts across barriers. When we've been given Christ himself, we have abundance. How could we ever afford to not be generous when he's given us all things?

PRACTICES

of Generosity

1. *Evaluate.* Ask yourself, When have I been generous to be seen by others or because it's the acceptable thing to do? Second, evaluate your schedule and budget. How much money and time do you give away?

2. *Meditate on "God gave."* Consider John 3:16 as you wake up each day. What does it mean for God to give his only son for you? Pray the Spirit would awaken the eyes of our heart to grow in gratitude.

3. *Pray to feel needy.* Ask God to show you your neediness and the needs of your neighborhood. Ask him to break your heart for your sin and for the things that break his heart. In repentance and faith, move forward and invite others to feel their needs alongside you.

4. *Tithe your money and your time.* Prayerfully consider what you could cut to make space for increased generosity. Ask God to provide opportunities for you to engage a neighbor in conversation, find local needs, and seek to meet them. Give to your local church. Ask where you can be involved in what God is already doing in your community.

5. *Commit to a habit that hurts.* It's easy to give our cast-offs. Start with a discipline that you can feel the weight of: fasting, tithing, volunteering, protesting, and babysitting are a few starter ideas.

9

The Opportunity of Cul-de-sacs

VULNERABILITY

Vulnerability is not weakness. . . .
It is the birthplace of creativity, innovation and change.

BRENÉ BROWN, 2012 TED TALK

ALL OF OUR CHILDREN'S BIRTHS have been dramatic in different ways. Our third birth started routinely enough—contractions in the bathtub in the middle of the night, leaving home before the other children awoke, and pacing the hospital halls to speed up labor. In the dead of a Utah winter, I shuffled in snow boots around waiting room furniture, stopped to breathe through the vicelike squeeze that would radiate to an ache in my tailbone, and then my husband would put his body weight into relieving the back pain by pressing into the pain. Camden, it turned out, was sunny side up (hence the back pain).

In the delivery room he was slow in coming. While my first son, Ezra, was birthed through an emergency C-section, my second son, Porter, had come minutes after we arrived in the hospital. I was still wearing my sandals and sundress in San Diego when he came flying into this world. But Camden, this soon-to-be-born third son, was quite content to stay put.

After a slow labor, I was exhausted and exposed. A hospital gown for covering; a team of labor and delivery nurses to bring cold washcloths, help hold my legs, and let me dig my fingers into their palms; and a doctor coaching me to push. But I couldn't. I just wanted to go to sleep. We were stuck.

The doctor rolled up a towel lengthwise to make a rope and gave me an end. He and I were now playing tug-of-war. This was how I was going to push this baby out. All I had to do when the next wave hit was to pull on my end of the towel, curve my back like a C while the nurses pulled my legs back and I placed every bit of fear, tiredness, and desperation into the fibers of that hospital towel.

"*Ah*, my back!" I howled, my nose wrinkling and my mouth widening in a lion-like pant. I'd stop, catch my breath. Bryce would cheer me on, scrubs on and waiting to catch his third boy.

"*Oh!*" I wailed, the crescendo moving up, then plummeting down in exhaustion. It was part victory cry, part defeat. The only words I had were exhaustion, but there was no rest. There was only the bearing up under the pain, with people I knew who could help carry it for me. There were the low, guttural cries of power that would burst forth loud and clear, and then, just as quickly, die out in an intake of breathless gasping. This is how birth happens—through nakedness, exposure, in practicing presence through pain.

> This is how birth happens—
> through nakedness,
> exposure, in practicing
> presence through pain.

For a birthing mother descends to death and finds a primal power there; on the other side, she is changed. Her body has borne suffering, sometimes flaggingly and sometimes boldly, yet she often finds an unknown strength. Birthing is an accomplishment of not knowing she was capable of so much joy, sadness, fear, failure, and pain all wrapped together. It is embodying the joy set before her that she relaxes again and again and bears down through it all.

Whether we birth our children through our own bodies, make a family through adoption, or stand waiting to become parents—in short, when we extend our bodies and souls to welcome more people into the community of our family—we must make peace with pain and the risk of profound loss. We must become vulnerable. Vulnerability only happens in the community and for its good. Vulnerability is inescapable for relationships to flourish.

BIRTHING VULNERABILITY

The language of birth is the best one I know to capture the paradox of vulnerability: this combination of strength and fragility, of bravery and fear, of the need for internal resources and a supportive community, and how when we let go we're actually making the most progress. The language of birth also informs how Brené Brown describes vulnerability: "vulnerability is the birthplace of creativity, innovation and change." Vulnerability is a messy, complicated birthing process.

Like my own births, sometimes vulnerability is unsure and scary, or so fast that your body and mind aren't caught up to one another, or tedious and ineffective, and even unexpectedly laced with joy, sorrow, laughter, and pain. But for each birth, at the moment when a mother thinks she'll break in half, where she can't go one step further, the baby is closest to being born. So too for all of us: when we are at our most vulnerable, we are often on the cusp of being born into something new and glorious.

In vulnerability, we are both the birthing mother and the baby unsure of what is happening. As mother, we do the next thing—we may not know what's coming, but we practice breathing to open up our bodies and souls for the pain and the unknown. We stay present. We bear up together under pain. In this analogy, as child, we are wrenched from our comfortable womb of safety and forced into the harshness of bright light and sound. But we are meant for life outside the womb, even if it is there where we will both wound and be wounded.

Thinking of vulnerability through the language of birth gives it a communal richness that vulnerability as emotional exposure loses. When we think of ourselves as vulnerable, it's usually of the secret-spilling variety. Andy Crouch, in his book *Strong and Weak*, helpfully widens the definition to mean "exposure to meaningful risk." An emotionally charged, truthful conversation can embody meaningful risk, but it can also be manipulative, using intimacy not to extend ourselves for others but to make ourselves heard or feel better. When we use our emotional vulnerability not in service to others but for ourselves, we are consumers of human relationships.

The problem is that in the suburbs most of our lives are lived behind physical, emotional, and spiritual gates and closed doors, where, when we do emerge, we oscillate between making even our mess look picture-perfect or we lose our boundaries all together. Like the shape of a cul-de-sac, we need part of us to be open and unguarded, while there must be a corresponding u-shaped harbor of safety. Vulnerability isn't boundary-less, but neither is it impenetrable. Ultimately, when we choose vulnerability it must be for the benefit of another.

If it's more than emotional transparency, what does vulnerability look like? It can be emotional disclosure when it helps another person feel known and seen. Vulnerability happens when a leader exposes her weakness, not to be a rags to riches story, but to help her followers. Vulnerability is laced throughout the Old Testament when prophets boldly spoke truth to power. We're embodying vulnerable risk when we stay humble and yet still show up to protest or support a friend at a court hearing. We're vulnerable when we walk alongside someone, helping them slowly through the learning process, without bulldozing them because we value results and our time more. Vulnerability means initiating hard conversations (or being on the receiving end of one) by asking someone to change course or repent, or by gently pointing out self-centered habits of sin, because life is richer as we align our lives with Christ. When vulnerability is for others and not for ourselves, it is always birthed through pain.

When we open ourselves up for meaningful risk, we risk loss. To return to our birth analogy, I remember our birthing instructors telling my husband about "transition": they said that when she says she can't do it anymore or feels like she's going to split in half, you need to tell her she *is* doing it. We embody vulnerability when we open ourselves up to pain, to the possibility of what feels like soul-crushing loss—and we bear up under it.

Why would we open ourselves up to such loss? Brené Brown writes that if we want to experience joy but cut ourselves off from pain, "we can't selectively numb emotion." To be fully human and not numb ourselves, we must find growth on the other side of loss, risk, and pain. It's the way of Jesus too.

The author of Hebrews describes Jesus taking on meaningful risk through his descent into suffering on the cross: "For the joy set before him he endured the cross, scorning its shame, and sat down at the right hand of the throne of God" (Hebrews 12:2 NIV). Jesus despised the cross's sin, shame, and humiliation for joy. What is that joy? The cross accomplishes the justification of sinners such as you and me. So Jesus moved into vulnerability and willful repudiation of his authority to accomplish salvation for others. In turn, vulnerability is a gift we offer to increase human flourishing of individuals, yes, but more than that, of entire communities.

Is vulnerability worth the risk? When we're comfortably curved inward, happy binge-watching Netflix and living on takeout between our children's sports practices, how can we catch a vision of human flourishing? How can we show others our broken selves for others— for their own growth and good? How can we choose to move forward— to square our shoulders and release our tendency to run away and curve inward? We have a guide, a wounded healer who has gone before us. We can only be vulnerable because we follow the man of sorrows, who has borne our pain and been tempted in every way (Hebrews 4:15). Jesus shows us a way forward. It just may look quite different than we imagine.

THE SELF-EMPTYING

I'd decided I was going to live in a snow globe. I'd bought cozy blue flannel pajamas in preparation for the quiet hush of snow softly falling outside the window where my last baby would be born in Utah. Newborn Harriet and I would curl up in the hospital bed together and watch the snowfall, just like I had with Camden's birth. I'd breathe in her newborn scent and enjoy a few days respite from packing lunches, monitoring naps, and enduring sibling bickering. That was how it was supposed to go.

Instead, an infection landed her in the Neonatal Intensive Care Unit. The halls became my labyrinth. I groggily made my way from the maternity ward in my blue polka-dot pajamas to the NICU. Days later, the path felt worn and the alarm on my phone became a familiar intrusion. I would make my way down one hall, then another, to the elevator, down a hall, and sign in to feed my baby. My breasts were heavy.

She looked like Gulliver, strapped down with wires, but with a purple bow glued to her head. There was no soft snowfall under the fluorescent lights. But I held her. I sang. I used my body to feed her. That was the only offering I had. The nurses loved her with a gentleness that felt angelic, more pure than my own mothering: a fusion of love, sacrifice, disappointment, exhaustion, and the smell of milk.

Yet I kept my routine with the reverence of liturgy. I moved every three hours to feed her, and then pumped out my milk in-between times so I could skip a middle-of-the-night journey and maybe get a few more hours of sleep. This, I told myself, was not supposed to happen. With the advent of our last surprise baby—a girl after three boys—everything was supposed to be new. She'd embody words I'd written before I was a mother; she'd be that darling girl with bouncing curls. Everything would be blanketed with hope.

But hope was in my trudging. It was my shuffling, slippered feet down sterile halls. It was my movement toward another human being down three floors lying in a plastic bed with an IV wire attached to her head. That was the movement of vulnerability—not in being curled in on ourselves like an impenetrable duo ("No, leave us alone; we're fine. This is my fourth baby. I've got it covered, thanks."), but in its opposite: in the movement outward. Each step down the hall, I gave up all that this was supposed to be and embraced what was. My power given for the sake of the sustenance of another. My plans dashed for the person in front of me, the littlest one with a purple bow. It felt of course a bit like death, because in some manner it was, even if a small death to those "hyphenated sins of the human spirit."

As people of faith, we can expose ourselves to meaningful risk—with all its accompanying beauty and brokenness—because we have a God-man who has gone before us, who has triumphed over death itself, and who is our perfect parent. This one who is with us now through his Spirit is not the lofty grandfatherly god shaking his head at us. He trudges down hospital halls offering himself. He is the father standing at the end of the road, running with robes lifted when his boy comes home. He is the father who goes out to meet his stubborn firstborn. He welcomes us into his feast.

We don't have to earn it: it is the pure welcome of hospitality. We don't have to be entrapped in cycles of self-justification or busyness, but we can venture out on faulty shaking legs and try on vulnerability. Then we know in our bones our worth isn't contingent on what others think of us, how we perform, what we earn, or what we have. That is the freedom of blessed self-forgetfulness, and when we have it because we are God's beloved, we're free to make mistakes. We can embrace meaningful risk because we know we are held.

We can take heart that Jesus went to the desert alone, fasting and praying. There he was tempted with ease, comfort, self-sufficiency, and status—

> **We can embrace meaningful risk because we know we are held.**

suburbia's "preciouses." At every turn his stomach probably grumbled and his spirit likely trembled, but the unchanging and faithful Word used the word of the triune God to place himself in a position of risk, not for his own aggrandizement but ultimately in service for others.

Jesus risked temptation, but it culminated in his own descent into suffering; Jesus was separated from God and took on our sin and shame so we would never be separated from God. This descent into suffering is the self-emptying that vulnerability requires.

We have a God who will never leave us or forsake us, so we can walk through small and large acts of suffering and emerge whole. We can bear a small cross because Jesus bore his and bears ours with us. This ability to bear up under hardship, suffering, and risk vulnerability is a chorus we hear echoed throughout Scripture, not just in Jesus' temptation in the wilderness. It is this: because of the presence of God, we are free to extend ourselves in vulnerability for the flourishing of others.

Risk means that loss is possible, perhaps inevitable as we journey toward suffering and powerlessness. The cry of vulnerability echoes Daniel's friends—Shadrach, Meshach, and Abednego—when they refused to worship the political leader Nebuchadnezzar, and the punishment was death by fire. They replied, "If we are thrown into the blazing furnace, the God we serve is able to deliver us from it, and he will deliver us from Your Majesty's hand. But *even if* he does not, we want you to know, Your Majesty, that we will not serve your gods or worship the image of gold you have set up" (Daniel 3:17-18 NIV, emphasis mine). The good news is held in that small phrase "even if."

We have a God who is truth and love, who bore our sin—all the ways we are turned in ourselves and twist good gifts into self-service. This God is the one who meets us in fire, in poverty, in suffering. We find that as we choose to expose ourselves to meaningful risk, we open ourselves up increasingly to experience God's presence.

Conversely, when we barricade our souls by surrounding ourselves with feather pillows and rich food, and when we seek wholeheartedly after the suburban dream, we will never know there is a deep hunger that can only be met by the Word who dwells with us, even through risk, even in pain.

It is always at the intersection of power and weakness where we find the God-life. Paul writes of the meaningful risk Jesus took on when he "emptied himself, by taking the form of a servant, being born in the likeness of men" (Philippians 2:7). But this self-emptying, or *kenosis*, of Jesus isn't simply a nice theological word to connote how Christ emptied himself of some of his divine characteristics to become human. Hak Joon Lee writes of *kenosis* as "the surrendering of a space," particularly the space of privilege within the church. This is the risk for suburban Christians. Therefore, Lee writes, "Paul is directly telling them to exemplify servanthood by 'giving space' to others as Jesus did rather than holding on to power and privilege." Vulnerability in the suburbs must be the process where we make room, privileging accommodation for others in our time, our homes, and our hearts.

CUL-DE-SACS AND THE CHURCH

Vulnerability requires both exposure and necessary boundaries. In the suburbs, vulnerably living from faith requires a commitment to both the local church and our neighborhoods. In both places, we need spaces of safety and spaces of risk. Our suburban neighborhood planning gives us a helpful image in the cul-de-sac.

In its shape as both open and closed, cul-de-sacs actually promote neighborliness. Thomas Hochschild's sociological research shows the benefits of cul-de-sacs: "Build cul-de-sacs where neighbors might develop that social cohesion, . . . and more people may watch out for each other, and feel less alone or alienated. . . . People who know their immediate neighbors are also more likely to care about and become involved with their neighborhood at a larger scale." That is, when our houses are oriented toward one another, our contact naturally increases. We become involved in each other's lives, watch each other's children, share a cup of flour, listen when a neighbor is worn down or hurting. Suburban geography—when we slow down enough to use it well—actually fosters community. Our streets are less busy; we just need to start walking them, and standing in our cul-de-sacs to meet other people and grow relationships.

We belong to each other with the barking dogs, quirky couples, crazy kids, and differing work schedules. We belong to our place: the driveways, alleyways, neighborhood walking paths, and common third spaces where we bump into one another. When we belong to each other and our place, we become community. But to move beyond the surface neighborliness of the cul-de-sac to a flourishing community, we must do more than ask for and borrow an egg when we're out—we must extend ourselves toward others through vulnerability. If our actual cul-de-sacs promote neighborliness, what are we doing with them? How are we extending ourselves in small acts of vulnerability that grow outward? What is the purpose of our vulnerability?

As we work at neighborliness, extending ourselves into positions of meaningful risk is not for self-promotion, work promotions, or an emotional hit we feel when we unburden ourselves. That is simply using someone made in God's image to get what we want. Vulnerability is always about the flourishing of a community. It's why at home my husband and I speak about being a part of a family versus following each child's propensities, wishes, whims, and desires at any given moment. It's not that an individual's giftedness doesn't matter, but that they find their proper place when they are housed within communities—from the family, to the neighborhood, to the church. Flourishing happens only within the context of vulnerable community.

> Flourishing happens only within the context of vulnerable community.

For the Christian, this community is not only the family or neighborhood, but also primarily the local church. The church, with all its brokenness, failure, and mixed-up motives, is still Christ's bride. Yet it seems commitment to a life of discipleship in the church feels increasingly optional for many in the suburbs.

Even so, to live faithfully in the suburbs means we commit to our local church and our neighborhoods. When our church is vulnerably living out a life of faith in our neighborhoods, it's natural to invite friends into a life of following Jesus. When the church is for the needs of its neighborhood, then it, as a living organism, gives up its authority for the good of those it serves. This starts with us. It starts with us finding a safe harbor in the u-shape of the church so we can move out to our actual cul-de-sacs.

We're quick to make church into a check box, the thing we do on Sunday morning when we commute to church to find our perfect fit, like a perfect pair of jeans. Church is not another consumer choice. "Church is not meant to be a 'customizable Christian experience' but an entrance into the Being and act of God here and now." If the call to hospitality is to start small and stay put, the call to learning vulnerability is to begin to practice it in the local church. There our vulnerability will propel us to worship, to lives of obedience, and to take on risk for the good of others.

It's often easier to be vulnerable in the confines of social media, email, or a text to a college roommate. Such moves are boundaried and calculated. It's quite another thing to apologize to your neighbor for your behavior Friday night, to release neighborhood grudges, to encourage people at church even if you voted differently from one another, and to continue in a life of repentance together.

If we want to find holy in the suburbs, it's got to start with the church and move through our cul-de-sacs. It starts with individual members practicing vulnerability together. As the church serves its neighborhood, the church vulnerably empties itself for the good of the community. If Jesus died for the church, and we are a group of sinners saved by grace, the church should be the easiest place to begin growing

FINDING HOLY IN THE SUBURBS

in vulnerability. Often, sadly, it is the opposite. If you're aching for your own church and neighborhood to be a place of authenticity, risk, and vulnerability, where there is more than polite nods while you pass neighbors in their SUVs or meet over coffee at church, then turn that prickly feeling inward: you go first. That is the essence of leadership. To belong to others and our places builds us into neighbors.

Here's a bit of what that looks like in our church plant in the suburbs: we have seen stoic men start to verbalize their doubts and see God meeting their fears. We've seen people whose tendency is to withdraw or run away when it gets hard to stay put. We've seen men and women verbalize the relational dysfunction of their past and ask for help. We've seen people who hadn't opened a Bible in years start to read it and begin to serve. We've seen taco parties and Christmas parties and meals of takeout pizza and wine bring the neighborhood to church. We've seen the gospel actually make sense to people and their whole lives change.

Most of all, I've seen my husband (who's not the empathetic crier I am) stand up to preach Sunday after Sunday not knowing how each sermon will land, tenderly loving the people in front of him, tearing up as he talks about the goodness of the gospel and gently exposing his own failures. Afterward, he's emotionally spent and exhausted, because he has given his life away every week. He both craves feedback and knows it will never be enough. He is learning the path of gently and tenderly leading his flock like the good Shepherd who goes before him, who carries his (like each of ours) sin, failure, shame, need for approval, brokenness, and vulnerability. When you begin to get a vision for finding holy in the suburbs, you must often be the one who offers yourself first, the one who goes first, who bears the first pain.

Vulnerability happens as we bear the pain of leadership. It isn't always pretty: we've been on the receiving end of hard conversations about hurt and pain, where we choose to dig in, not blame or cut and run. I've pounded fists on the steering wheel of my minivan at a loss for words, not knowing how to speak truth in love, but knowing it must be stumbled through as best as I could. Vulnerability is hard, tender, and awkward work.

Vulnerability hurts, yes—but this is exactly how we grow. Like birth, there is much pain in vulnerability: its end is unknown, its pain new and different each time we try it on. But also like birth, it is a pain for a purpose. Only through birth do we truly live. Only through vulnerability do we begin to flourish and work toward shalom in our neighborhoods and world. How can we be content with busyness or bigger houses when there is so much more? Is there any greater hope than living a life belonging to a people and place where we are free to fail and free to flourish? Is there any greater hope than living for something beyond ourselves, our success, or our children's security?

We know we're vulnerable. Yet most days we choose to hide it with busyness or what we buy, or conversely we share all of our problems so our vulnerability is only about us. The church offers blessed relief from needing to have it all together. We join a family of sinners, all saved by grace, where we practice the hard work of vulnerability. It doesn't stop there: we welcome our neighborhoods into this life where we don't have to perform or fake feeling fine. We get to bring the unfettered welcome of Jesus into our cul-de-sacs.

PRACTICES

of Vulnerability ⟵

1. *Take stock.* Notice where you resist "meaningful risk" (whether that's in conflict, emotion, desire, or something else) and pray through your list.

2. *Make a list of safe people.* Practice a small risk first with those who are safest to you. Schedule a conversation. Pray to extend your vulnerability for the sake of others.

3. *Stay curious.* Ask good questions about those you're already in relationship with. Also extend yourself to neighborhood thought leaders, local government, artists, and homeowners' association employees.

4. *Commit to the church.* Make weekly church-going a priority for three months. Look for one way each week you can practice meaningful risk in your local congregation by volunteering, having a hard conversation when it's necessary, joining a small group, or meeting new people.

5. *Find neighborhood watering holes.* Find the places where people congregate. Awkwardly hang out there and ask simple questions to get to know your neighbors. Give yourself a month where you walk to your local school with your children and begin to develop relationships with your neighbors. Pray these relationships move toward vulnerability.

10

Paper Birds and Human Flourishing

SHALOM

Just as Jesus is the embodiment of the shalom *that God intends for creation, the church's role in the drama of Creation is likewise to be the embodiment of God's* shalom, *albeit in a form that hasn't yet been fully realized.*

C. Christopher Smith and John Pattison, *Slow Church*

MY TWO LITTLE CURLY-HAIRED BOYS waited eagerly to see the monarchs released from our butterfly kit. We'd watched the caterpillars grow like sponges, puffed up with food, until they began to grow sluggish. When the directions specified, we moved them to a larger habitat, a mesh cylinder where they'd attach and build their chrysalises. In the burgeoning spring, we brought them along for a family vacation in search of sun—the butterfly habitat carefully placed on top of suitcases and kept warm. Their chrysalises were hard and brown. They looked like tightly closed attaché cases from a period drama, the ones that fit everything neatly in a click closed with a gold lock. They quivered at the top of the mesh cage, and one day, they cracked open in new birth.

Their wings were sticky and brown, not the glorious fluttering of orange monarchs. But in the following days, they grew bright and strong. They opened and closed their wings soundlessly as they stared back at my boys' eager laughter in their bright eyes, my boys watching the wonder of creation in front of their preschool noses. The butterflies were ready for release—all except one. One small suitcase of a chrysalis had tried to crack open, but stopped midway. It had since fallen and stayed motionless at the bottom of the cylinder.

We opened the mesh zipper to let out the ones who'd made the change from small caterpillar to flit their wings in glory for a few weeks before they too would return to dust. My boys chased them around the yard, shouting and pointing as they'd land on a flower, whooping when they soared off into the tree branches that bent over our picket fence. The light caught their wings and hope grew there too, especially in a butterfly that lingered a bit longer. I wondered how one could just fly off like that, unknowing.

My children took it all in: the feeding caterpillars, the waiting as they turned in on themselves into chrysalises, the delight when we'd come home and find one had broken free and become something else entirely—a creature of wonder and grace, its wings opening and closing silently. They even took in stride the one that never opened.

But I fretted over that one almost-butterfly that died in the great exchange. What could I do? Change the temperature? Help him out in any way when he began to crack open his chrysalis? But everything I'd read said not to touch: our fingerprints might change their wings; what we thought would aid their flight would be their grounding. So he remained a broken butterfly at the bottom of a mesh cage, and while my children danced along with the butterflies, a deep sadness radiated through my chest and settled in a lump in my throat.

This was not the way things were supposed to be.

SUBURBAN SUBSTITUTES FOR SHALOM

Perhaps we best know shalom by what it is not, by feeling deep in our bones that this—whatever *this* is—is not how the world is supposed to be. It is not home. We desire to be placed people: "Home represents humanity's most visceral ache—and our oldest desire," writes Jen Pollock Michel in *Keeping Place*. We know our loss of wholeness by the butterfly that never completes the transformation, by the baby who is never conceived, by the mental illness that keeps covering all the goodness, by the marriage that ended, by the child who turns his back. Our homes, our neighborhoods, and the news show us that inequality, unkindness, the pursuit of power for its own sake, and systemic oppression rule the day.

Although we are materially wealthy in the suburbs, we are spiritually poor. That is, we look to buy our way to wholeness rather than practice the robust habits that will enable our souls to stretch and extend ourselves for the good of our place rather than ourselves. We trade a life of rich meaning, purpose, and a love we needn't earn for suburban shortcuts. Affluence cannot bring wholeness. We cannot buy or work harder for shalom.

I have thought that with enough healthy eating, Bible reading, quiet time, and good sunshine, I would increasingly move toward wholeness. Yet, even on the days I check off my boxes for all those things, I find anger or disappointment wrapping itself around my heart and spewing forth at those I love. More good habits do not change hearts. Our spiritual muscles are weak.

We must name our privilege plainly: because of our material wealth (and often other forms of privilege) we don't feel our need for God. When our neediness breaks in, we run, distract, and offload. So we try to buy our way out of neediness. We distract ourselves from the state of our needy souls by staying busy. We do this in countless ways: we turn to things or the house to find home and belonging, or we work harder, sacrifice for our children, act responsibly, and let loose on the weekend. Because we do not need to worry for our safety or our sustenance, we have the privilege to pretend these problems don't exist for other people. We are blind to how our suburban privilege insulates us.

What we have amassed in the course of this "good life" of suburbia is a purely self-referential life. We have not extended ourselves for others—even our children can be simple accessories to our lives of privilege. In the suburbs the default setting is to fill our soul hungers with fast-food versions: things bought and sold, relationships orbiting around what they offer, love given to fill ourselves up or make us feel wanted and needed. Personal and communal wholeness is not birthed from hustle.

These days, of course, we can make idols out of people, places, and things, but we also may live lives so infinitely distractible that we can fail to be present to ourselves, our families, and the needs and desires of our neighbors. It is not that we need to worship at the altar of a career or even a white picket fence to move away from God, we just need to be attuned to the ding of our phones in our pockets—the next notification that will distract us from feeling the weight of our own homelessness. In the suburbs, we most often build sandcastles that will eventually fall and fade away, or we withdraw into worlds of distraction. There is a better way. Like grace, shalom is a gift and the home to which we are headed, even when we live in exile.

> Like grace, shalom is a gift and the home to which we are headed, even when we live in exile.

SHALOM AND THE GOSPEL

Sin is exile. It is a story of homelessness; yet the story of shalom starts within this story of exile. Kelton Cobb writes, "At the core of biblical narrative is the story of displacement—of having wandered a long way from home, and longing to return. This is the underlying plot of being cast out of Eden, of being foreigners in Egypt, of the journey to the promised land, of the losing of exiles in Babylon to return to the land of their fathers. . . . This plot of exile and return is the part of the deep structure of the Bible." And if we are Christians, no matter where and how we live, this is where our story starts too.

If sin exiles us, how we are we brought home? What is the vision for how things ought to be? The Bible answers "shalom." The Bible and theologians use rich language to speak about shalom. Cornelius Plantinga writes, "The webbing together of God, humans, and all creation in justice, fulfillment, and delight is what the Hebrew prophets call *shalom*."

Shalom is the word we reach for to talk about justice, mercy, and the God-honoring relationship between people, places, and things. It's the interconnectedness that we long for; it's the satiation of desire and longing; it's the proper relationship between earth, humankind, and our work. Our word *shalom* points to the acceptance, unity, peace, flourishing, and rightness of the created order that God originally intended and to which we are moving. Shalom can only grow from the fruit of lament and repentance, and from clinging to Christ who clothes us in his righteousness.

If sin exiles us, then shalom is the great story of the gospel and how wholeness and flourishing are rewoven. Shalom tells the gospel story in four acts: we were created for shalom, sin ruptures shalom, Jesus redeems shalom, and shalom is where we're headed. The gospel story of shalom is good news for exilic people.

Suburbanites are exilic people, not in the Hollywood trope that suburbia is a place where culture goes to die, or in the sense that we need to withdraw from the places in which we live and live disembodied "holy" lives. The biblical prophets speak of existential exile as the post-Edenic home of all people. Exile is not only our state of being but also the setting for God's shalom to come in and sweep us and our neighborhoods off our feet.

The Old Testament prophets write wildly of shalom breaking through exile, promising hope and a home for God's people. They speak about Eden being restored (Ezekiel 36:33-35), streams in the desert (Isaiah 35), the wolf lying down with the lamb (Isaiah 11:6-9), of tears and death being no more (Isaiah 65:19). As the good news of the gospel works in our hearts, it will work itself out more fully in our neighborhoods and churches. We will find ourselves caught in the tension of longing for heaven and being deeply committed to the work of the church in our hearts and cul-de-sacs. Shalom is more than *our* ultimate flourishing or peace—shalom is God himself.

> Shalom is more than *our* ultimate flourishing or peace—shalom is God himself.

This is key for the suburbs. This enables us to live in a Godward path no matter where we find ourselves. It also helps us to engage our privilege and learn how to lay it down and give it away.

˗ ☁ ☼ ☁ ˗

The first instance of God as our peace comes in the book of Judges, in Gideon's story. Gideon is faithful in battle and builds an altar, calling it Yahweh-Shalom, "the Lord Is Peace" (Judges 6:24). But we meet Gideon before that, when God's people are exiled and overrun. Gideon is threshing wheat in the middle of a winepress, a hiding place where he works under the constant watch of their captors, the oppressive Midianites.

Gideon's minding his own business, hiding out, when an angel of the Lord sees him in the winepress and calls him "man of valor"—not exactly the moniker we might choose for a man afraid. Yet this is precisely how Yahweh-Shalom works: infusing grace and truth backward into time and place. Gideon is a mighty warrior, even when he hasn't yet lived out his calling. He has done nothing to warrant "mighty warrior," but God sees and acts on our behalf outside time and space.

When addressed by the angel of God, Gideon's first reaction is surprise, and then he gets real: in Judges 6:13 he questions Israel's enslavement and asks, "Where is God? How can God be this great savior who brought us out from Egypt when here I am threshing wheat in a winepress, when we're victims of oppression?" (paraphrase). It's our question too: "Where is God if evil and calamity happens, and he does not rescue us?"

Rather than chastise him, the text says the Lord (Yahweh, yes, God himself) turned to Gideon and said, "Go in the strength you have and save Israel out of Midian's hand. Am I not sending you?" (Judges 6:14 NIV). Gideon, to be sure, executes a series of tests. He brings an offering of meat and unleavened bread. The stranger touches it with his staff and the offering is consumed. And then the angel of the Lord is gone.

When it becomes clear to Gideon that this angel is God himself, Gideon is rightfully terrified and worried he will die, for he cannot be in the presence of a holy God. The messenger speaks, "Peace!" Then, as the story unfolds, this terrifying holy God goes before him, magnificent and intimate, and Gideon drives out the Midianites. He later builds an altar and names it Yahweh-Shalom (Judges 6:24).

The good news of the gospel is not that God will bestow the pixie dust of shalom over your life or your circumstances. Shalom isn't about your feelings about God. The good news is that God himself will be your shalom in every place, in every nation, and in every culture.

As he does for Gideon, God will send us outward into our neighborhoods to fight for justice, to value God's image in every person, and to begin to work toward reconciliation. Through it all, God is the prize. He is our peace. And no fancy car, big house, mental acumen, emotional intelligence, or successful child will ever come close to the shalom that is God, who promises to never leave or forsake us.

LAMENT: THE MINISTRY OF PAPER BIRDS

When we experience Jesus as our peace, we are naturally brought to repentance for trying to sate our deep hungers with the fast-food fixes of the suburbs. When we repent, our hearts start to break for the ways we've insulated ourselves with our privilege, how we have not sought out the broken and needy, how we numb and distract ourselves from our own deep neediness. We've sought the sparkles of suburban life without using our time, bodies, and resources for the shalom of God's world.

We must open up space for lament in the suburbs so we can work toward shalom. This is the lesson I learned from my son, Porter, one spring morning. Porter called me out to our suburban patio, and with a joyful gesture he pointed out how he'd spied our mama bird up on the house next to ours. She had made a nest in a little pot on our patio; even strewn with weeds it had held her eggs for three seasons. I wondered why she wasn't watching over her eggs. I turned to look at our pots we'd just cleaned up yesterday in a Saturday morning spent weeding.

Her pot was missing. My stomach dropped. I got fidgety. *Where was the pot? Where were her babies?*

I ran around the house, trying to make sense of what happened and what could be done—*How could baby bird eggs be accidentally thrown away?*

I went to the source and when I could bear to peek, I peered into the trashcan. There the nest was nestled in the bottom of the green bin. There were no more eggs.

I stomped like a two-year-old, I slammed doors, I ugly cried. I hugged my husband and then pushed him away. I couldn't contain the sadness. I wanted to run forever. Then came the guttural sounds inches from my bedroom floor, echoes of the ones that had reverberated over a toilet I sat on a dozen years ago: "No! No! No! No! Not another baby lost!"

What was I supposed to say to a wee mama bird perched on the eaves of the house across from ours, who kept peering over, wondering where her babies had gone? How could I communicate that somehow we'd thrown away her babies? So I screamed and railed at the injustice of happenstance, at how cleaning up our patio turned us into death dealers.

I stomped, I yelled, I threw away our kitchen trash and opened up trash can liners until they billowed like angry clouds.

Meanwhile, my son Porter rushed to the couch, scissors in hand. I ran and collapsed on my bedroom floor, no words for the pain. A few minutes later, my son presented me with his gifts.

He took to paper and scissors when he saw ache, loss, and how broken the world is. He cut out and drew a mama bird and then a baby bird coming out of an egg—paper gifts handed to me with his outturned lip. He proceeded to create a bird family and unbroken paper eggs, and a baby bird that looked like a phoenix rising from the ashes. He dove right into my pain, anger, and confusion, and created art.

That is shalom. He saw pain and dove into its cracks, pointing me to something better, something that communicated deep sadness with a

> **He dove right into my pain, anger, and confusion, and created art.**

hint of redemption at its edges. Shalom in the suburbs dives into pain and makes paper birds.

Pain may look different in suburbia than homelessness, hunger, and insufficient resources, although those are there too. It looks like crippling debt behind closed doors. It looks like hidden poverty. It looks like microaggressions when you don't fit a dominant racial, ethnic, or socioeconomic mainstream. It looks like windows closed so wives and husbands can vent their rage. It looks like disconnection and emotional vacancy. It can even be an anesthetized version of safety, peace, and security when underneath we are not really living life. It looks like an outward presentation of manicured lawns while our souls grow lazy with our consumption, pride, and greed.

We have to know our neighbors and our own hearts well enough to ask hard questions and draw people out of hiding. We must practice vulnerably sharing our failures first and the goodness of Yahweh-Shalom to redeem our failures—to call us men and women of valor, even when we're hiding out.

But as in every place, our God who takes pain on for us can redeem our pain, or we can choose to fester in it and keep it close. When we've got a whiff of the release we have when Yahweh-Shalom takes our pain, we're free to actively work toward shalom.

THE CHURCH: AGENT OF SHALOM

After we confess and lament, what do we do to extend shalom in the suburbs? How do we ask hard questions; hold a neighbor's pain in cupped, outstretched hands; point them to Jesus; and work toward reconciliation in our suburbs? Please know this is not another thing to add to your to-do list. You are not responsible for being the sole neighborhood representative of shalom. This call is for the church, and you (as one member of that body) get to do your small part. Gideon's story helps me grasp hold of what it looks like to live out shalom in the suburbs.

We must start (like Gideon) to ask honest questions: Where is God now? Where is the church already active, already listening to the needs of its neighbors? Jump in there. God doesn't shame Gideon or us into working toward shalom; he invites us to participate in a grander story of freedom than accolades or numbers in a bank account.

Like Gideon being called "mighty warrior," you are an agent of shalom even if you have not lived it out, when you're hiding in your winepress. I'm often caught hiding. For me, it can feel safer to know things than to do things. I can share Facebook posts and read books when, for example, I've yet to volunteer with a local ministry my friends began that offers free tutoring to kids whose second (or third) language is English. Their families can't afford lessons. Their parents work multiple jobs just to survive. In response, my friends have opened their garage for free tutoring each afternoon. I've been content to pray occasionally, to wonder how I might get involved when I have four small children of my own. My lack of volunteering has less to do with the logistics of childcare and more to do with my fear that if I do help, I'll do it all wrong. I'll do it to ease a guilty conscience. I'll do it so I look good. I'll do it because I've felt the pressure to try to be present everywhere and do everything. So I'm no longer ignoring. I'm pausing and praying about my calling and where and how to serve. That is the first step out of hiding. I may be sent elsewhere, but I am not called to hide behind my fear or privilege and do nothing.

Friend, if you hide like me, or need time to pray about your hiding, we are still sent as agents of shalom. God calls us and asks us to fling open doors of welcome. You as an individual or family do not need to meet all the needs of your neighborhood. This is the call to the church. If this ministry is not my calling now, I can still connect others to it, give, pray for them, and ask how God can best use my time, talents, and family.

The call to shalom is not to just my local congregation either. Since our church is just getting started, we also partner with other churches— like when I spent a fall morning sorting donations with other moms (our children frolicking around piles of clothes) to be boxed and sent to refugee camps. These moments can feel too inconsequential to be important, but this is how shalom snowballs, in all the small ways when we lay down our lives for others.

Also, like Gideon, like Jesus, you are offered. Even if what you have to offer is small, it still costs you. It may not be grand world-changing words or actions. You may offer a hug for a hurting neighbor or prayer for your friend with chronic illness, a phone call to a government representative about their policies, or your presence in the midst of grief. Your offering can be feeding the neighborhood kids and giving them a kitchen island to hang out at. Being an offering is seeing the brokenness of the world and fashioning paper birds in small daily ways. We bake brownies for the awkward neighborhood kids. We invite a lonely friend for a drink. We don't hide from pain, awkwardness, and suffering. Flourishing is only found on the other side of sacrifice.

To be an offering day by day, we fight to stay present. For me, most of my days are spent mothering my four small children. I work to stay present for them—looking them in the eyes, helping them navigate their feelings, and giving them language for a world that is bigger than their desires or one that they only come to self-referentially.

This means I offer my time: we sit down weekly and write to our Compassion International child in Burkina Faso, we gather cans for a local food drive, and along with our church members we donate diapers to a teen pregnancy center. We have people in our home weekly for dinner. I may not be traveling to feed the homeless in this season, and that is okay. I know others in the church who do. In my corner of the suburbs, we are still learning habits that extend beyond our nuclear family and offer sustenance to our suburb.

Also, as an offering to your suburb, you will have to die. Your dreams of the good life will have to be swallowed up into the sweeter story of the gospel, whose narrative arc never has us at its center, but God alone.

Every other thing and idea you serve in the suburbs—safety, success, self-provision, self-actualization, productivity—will put you on a treadmill that never ends. There will always be safer fences for you to erect to protect you and yours physically and emotionally.

> Your dreams of the good life will have to be swallowed up into the sweeter story of the gospel, whose narrative arc never has us at its center, but God alone.

As we find ourselves within God's story, we are free to love God for what he has done for us and his presence with us. We then are also free to love others, not for what they can offer us but because they are fellow image bearers. We are free to love and disciple our children because they too are God's children like us, rather than focusing on fixing their behavior or giving in to their desires of the moment.

Dying to ourselves often looks quite ordinary: going to church weekly, having people over when I'd sometimes rather be by myself, beginning conversations about faith, how we spend our money, choosing to say I'm sorry, or specifically giving up my time to volunteer at our church's summer Kids Camp and Parents Night Out (a night of free babysitting in our community). These are the habits and practices that orient my heart outward, toward loving others and pursuing the peace of my suburb.

Through it all God, who is shalom, will be with you. We fight in-justice, envy, covetousness, the worship of busyness, individualism, and consumerism not with more knowledge but with the gospel of Yahweh-Shalom. We confess. We lament. We cry out to God in our pain, con-fusion, fear, and distraction. We cry out on behalf of our neighbors.

Again the practices of orienting our hearts toward Yahweh-Shalom are small: we read our Bibles; we pray together on a weekday afternoon for the needs of our church and community; we praise God's goodness and experience his presence in our worship services; we meet to en-courage one another in faith; we give our time and our money away so we are not dependent on them but on God. When we experience the presence of God with his people, we are able to be, like Paul, content in whatever situation we find ourselves, no matter the size of our family, our homes, or our paychecks (Philippians 4:11-13).

We can learn from Gideon that God provides, that he will give us all we need. When Gideon fought the Midianites, God whittled down his army from thirty-two thousand to three hundred so the victory against Midian could be none other than the Lord's. When our churches preach self-actualization and self-help, when our homes are large, our bank ac-counts steady, and our beauty the key to belonging, we position ourselves as heroes to our own life story. When instead God leads us into smallness, we not only see that our gains our God's alone, but also we begin to have eyes to see others. There we extend ourselves as peacemakers.

For example, when we began to make our suburban home, which once felt cramped and too small to host people from my church, our own—painting it, changing light fixtures, and dreaming about renovations—it became not a status symbol but a vehicle to love people and welcome them in. It wasn't just a fresh coat of paint. This home was the answer to my prayers that God would give us the home that we *need*—not the home that I even necessarily wanted.

I knew he could provide the large house up the hill, that God de-lights to give his children good gifts and isn't stingy with his blessings.

But I also knew my own heart and its tendency to elevate God's good blessings into what is worshiped rather than the Giver. I knew that ultimately I needed a home to be part of my practice of the presence of finding holy in the suburbs. My home was part of my offering, not yet another thing to buttress my own comfort.

In that way, God is merciful to show me again that he alone, not my square footage, is my comfort. It isn't just our desires, it's our pain (and the pain of our places) too: we bring broken hallelujahs to the throne of grace where we have a Man of Sorrows who sits with us in pain and who will one day entirely redeem the world twisted by sin. We have a Savior who has been the offering and gone through exile, all to bring us home. Glory, hallelujah.

SEEK THE SHALOM OF YOUR SUBURB

Your suburb is not your home. It is your place you are called to in exile as you wait for glory.

The call of shalom is to maintain, in James Davison Hunter's phrase, "faithful presence within" the structures of our neighborhoods and culture, as we experience God's presence even in exile. Just like God's people exiled in Babylon, we are not at home: "exile was the place where God was at work." Hunter continues, "As they pursued the shalom of Babylon, God would provide shalom for his people." If we can apply this to our context, it could read, "As we pursue the shalom of the suburbs, God will be our shalom, our peace. You are called to seek the shalom of your suburb."

Begin by imagining what needs your suburb has. What would it look like for the suburbs to flourish, to experience shalom? Suburbs are built on the premise of safety, comfort, and insulation. But safety is more than that—it's security that is deeper.

Experiencing shalom, suburbs would evidence strong marriages and stalwart communities. Children would be safe and free, and yet live for more than the latest gadget or what they could acquire. Imagine children growing up in safety, but not a safety borne from walling out others who aren't like us. Imagine people working hard, not for their beach vacation but for the good of the community. Imagine a tight-knit community where we valued our particularities and differences, we knew each other's names, and we saw needs and sought to meet them. Imagine homes flung open in hospitality, not traded in for bigger and better. Imagine a community where it was safe to be broken, where kindness was the first word, where privilege and affluence bred generosity, justice, and humility not simply for that community's sake but for the communities around it. Wouldn't that be a revolution in the suburbs?

Then imagine how the church is called to hold out the hope of the gospel and live it out in your suburb. Here's one small way our church is beginning to dream about meeting the deep need for safety in our community: we're brainstorming how to mobilize the gifts and knowledge of our people to offer free community classes on parenting in which we engage the culture of affluence, the influence of technology, and how parents can stay connected to their children in a culture of busyness. We hope that we'll be able to start discussions about how safety and success shouldn't be turned inward: instead, families would use safety and socioeconomic and racial privilege to move outward—to bring others in, create friendships, and use their power and authority not to puff themselves up but to actually help create a culture of flourishing for all people.

Be purposeful in your place: whether you move to a needier spot in your suburb or commit to staying put, or even keep an old car. As agents of shalom, we dig our hands in: we build houses and plant gardens. We commit to lives of vulnerability and hospitality—not to bigger is better—because Jesus did that. We say yes for the long haul to a particular people and place. When we attach ourselves to a place, writes Kathleen Norris, we "surrender to it, and suffer with it." That means that, yes, we suffer with the suburb's idols and idiosyncrasies.

But we also hold out hope for a life of abundance that isn't defined by working harder. It means we can exhibit the shalom of God in our contentment and help others get off the moving walkway of hustling for their worthiness. We do this in countless small ways. We invite people into our homes. We engage difference with compassion and questions, not condescension. We ask for eyes to see all the ways our affluence blinds us.

Then we take one small step. I easily get overwhelmed with the state of racial, social, and economic injustice, and I feel powerless to change anything. The call to be radical and world-changing can stifle any small ways we work out shalom in our neighborhoods. Boldly, Sarah Arthur and Erin F. Wasinger write in *The Year of Small Things*: "When we begin to dream about our cities, we must not fool ourselves that 'acts of kindness' suffice." It's true; it's easy to cover ourselves with the soft blanket of do-gooderism without actually doing the hard work of lament, confession, and uprooting injustice like a stubborn tree root that won't break loose.

But, it must be said, these acts of kindness may be how shalom in the suburbs starts. Acts of kindness are not the sum and substance of shalom, but they may be one baby step we take to begin to see others. We must start small and start somewhere if we're not going to be overwhelmed and do nothing.

It is our joy to be bringers of shalom in our suburbs; it overflows from the belovedness offered us in Jesus. As Osheta Moore writes at the end of her book *Shalom Sistas*, "Let us run, skip, jump, twirl, and dance all the way home, for we are practitioners of a subversive joy." This subversive joy will work itself out in countless acts of compassion, solidarity, and extension of ourselves for those who are different from us.

As you create habits of smaller "acts of kindness"—as you sit down to family dinner more often than not, as you open up your home to neighbors and neighborhood children, as you donate your time and money, as you dream with others about what your suburb would look like redeemed—your vision extends. We begin to see those on the margins. We see the homeless man who we've been driving by. We see the person of color who steps into our white church and we make an effort to offer welcome. We ask, Who's excluded because of their race, or who has no access because of their class, gender, or ability? Who isn't seen because they don't look right, sound right, or have the right education or house? Then, as we embody and practice the welcome of Christ, we don't just react to those on the margins, but we learn to move toward the marginalized, the broken, and the invisible.

The call to the suburban Christian is to wake up. And if God isn't calling you elsewhere, we stay put. We start small. We don't settle for the absence of conflict as an indication of peace. We instead seek the flourishing of our place and all the people—prominent and invisible— who are our neighbors. May we extend mercy in the suburbs; may we not be "more devoted to 'order' than to justice; . . . prefer[ing] a negative peace which is the absence of tension to a positive peace which is the presence of justice," as Dr. Martin Luther King Jr. wrote in his "Letter from a Birmingham Jail."

May we not be lulled into the suburban sin of complacency because we have the privilege to be complacent. May we always move forward, not to seek justice for justice's sake but more than that: to extend mercy and flourishing to all because that is how God has come to us—a Father running to us in welcome.

He has called you women and men of valor even when you're hiding in your winepress. As we are changed by his gospel, he shapes our lives into small offerings—little paper birds—of his work of redemption, presence, and mercy already at work in his church and the world. Amen.

PRACTICES

 **of Shalom**

1. *Pray for eyes to see.* Pray for God to show you the needs of your community. Pray to see the marginalized and how you can be a bridge to bring mercy, peace, and healing where you are.

2. *Realize you're not going to do it right, and do it anyway.* Pray for opportunities to work toward the peace of your suburb. When you sense a call, jump in. Seek to learn and work hard, but understand you're not going to do it all correctly. Love others and listen well.

3. *Seek to learn.* If the poor and marginalized have a great faith, seek to learn from them. Join a racial reconciliation group like Be the Bridge, volunteer at a local crisis pregnancy center, find a tutoring center or governmental agency where you can tithe your time. Ask questions—you are there to learn.

4. *Meditate.* Center your thoughts and prayers on what it means for Yahweh-Shalom to be with you as you seek the shalom of your suburb. Ask for guidance about his way forward for you, your family, and your community.

CONCLUSION

Coming Home

We will swallow God; we will drink God.
(And how sweet is the taste of the Divine!)

Julian of Norwich, *The Revelation of Julian of Norwich*

WHEN WE WERE INVITED TO the large estate of a generous philanthropist at Christmas, I spent a bit of time on what to wear. Should I opt for a dress from my closet, buy a new one, borrow a friend's, stay with my standard black, wear pantyhose or not?

After borrowing a friend's black dress and my mother's beaded clutch, and putting on my heels, we left for the night. After we arrived, with a glass of wine now in hand, we discovered the entire house was a library for art and books. We toured the grounds, chatted with guests, and stepped into room after room that, rather than soaring to the heights with an effort to make a person feel small, felt intimate, homey—small rooms to sit and read, a living room with a crackling fireplace and chairs for conversation, an intimate dining room in the wine cellar. At the designated time, we filed into the red-walled, double-doored dining room for a sit-down dinner for eighteen; there was an appropriate mix of the immanent with the transcendent. Crystal. Gold. Wood. Art that made me catch my breath. The table itself was glory.

The lights were low but the whole room glowed with candlelight bouncing off crystal, glass, red and gold. The table overflowed with flowers and candles scattered liberally, turning it into an undulating experience of petals and light. Tucked into corners were little ornaments from around the world that made my lips part in delight at the surprise of finding the hidden whimsy and artistry of it all. Course after delicious course came. Wine glasses were never empty. And the eighteen of us were asked to answer one simple question: When did you experience an event so transformative that you knew God was real?

I flushed when I heard it, and my stomach did that flip-flop it does when I know I must speak something true, something that hits at my marrow. What sort of stories would other people tell? Would I fall apart trying to tell my story of the specifics about my move home to the suburbs, that I've best known God in the giving up? How would that look?

The good thing about the gospel is that it enables us to let go of pretense. I stand alone by the story of a Father who runs to meet us in our shame, brokenness, and self-righteousness. My tears are not a liability.

The stories overflowed like wine: God had come near in suffering and healing—husbands bedridden, children lost, hope for adoption, and family reconciliation. But being stuck in the present tense of my story meant that all the emotion found its way out of my heart and into my body. When it was my turn, I found myself choking back tears in my borrowed black dress, as I recounted my story contained in these pages: this was not what I thought I wanted. I felt almost bred for glory—which seemed to be the American dream, success, living overseas—and then God broke in and humbled us, bringing us more children than we thought we could handle easily, and suddenly we were learning how to live the kingdom of God with our children not as accessories but as brothers and a sister in Christ. God also called us to start a church back home in the suburbs of our birth. For the move, every door had opened: financial provision, friends and the powers that be agreed this was God's good for us, and friends to move with us to plant the church. But still I felt more akin to Jacob, wrestling with God, than Mary, the one to birth the Son of God, who said "Let it be so."

What was first birthed in me was discontent, pain, and self-pity. Railing at the suburbs for its idols of consumerism, individualism, image, and a lifestyle that was too expensive to afford. Angry that I wanted it too. Angry that I'd ended up right back where I started instead of walking city streets, taking my children to art galleries, or chasing baby chicks in the countryside. I know deep down that no place will fully satisfy. That the cities and rural life are not escapes, just as my suburban one is not an escape from all that haunts us as human beings. But I desperately want it to be true. I want to escape to an idyll. I want to find myself contentedly at home.

But in his kindness, God has brought me low. He has lovingly exposed the ways I think myself superior or better than my place. He has shown me, in the pain of my own body, that I am but a breath. He has shown me how a life in the suburbs does not absent us from the problems of other places, even if the suburban idols fashioned here are different, more insidious, and harder to root out. Most of all God has shown me himself—in sunshine, in walks, in tenderness, in showing me that all places can point me home, all places can be appetizers of glory.

I've needed the immanence of God because I often expect glory to look lavish, like that table. And it does. I expect glory to show up in feasts around tables every time. But it also shows up in kind children, ordinary pots of soup shared in love, a night off, and a chance to do what makes me most come alive. Like their home, my generous hosts invited both a sense of God's grandeur and his intimate, listening ear. Their home could have had two-story ceilings, long hallways—spaces that distance owner from guest. The dinner could have been a chance to make good on their investments, check in on progress, make their own wishes clear so that they could steer culture. But it wasn't.

> It was grace, gift, and sacrament. It was a table set for a feast to bring all of us prodigals home.

That table, that night, were gifts—a foretaste of the marriage supper of the Lamb. It married the immanent and the transcendent; the broken with the beautiful. It was grace, gift, and sacrament. It was a table set for a feast to bring all of us prodigals home.

THAT'S HOW THE LIGHT GETS IN

The suburbs have it wrong insofar as we perpetuate a language of "world changing." The endless pursuit of success in work, fancy vacations, children who are on the honor roll and whose highest career aspiration is to be a professional sports player of some kind; we try to root glory in the here and now. We imagine our lives on a middle-class upward trajectory full of greater success, prestige, or at least increased opportunities than the previous generation.

There's an evangelical Christian version of "world changing" too. You had to do big things to show you were serious about God—in the last decade of the twentieth century, it meant wearing WWJD bracelets, witnessing to your friends at school, making sure you were "sold out" to God through emotionally moving worship experiences, and considering giving up your material advantages to serve God in Africa, or at least in downtown Los Angeles. But what do you do when your world looks nothing like you thought it would? What do you do when your days are filled with laundry and good but often tedious work, when you spend more time cleaning up after children than proclaiming the gospel? What do you do when you're trying to live for God in an average suburb?

We wait for the glory of God. Our lives are not meant to be ads for how good the gospel is, complete with shiny phrases and colors. Our chief task is not to change the world, but in the words of an old catechism on faith "to glorify God, and to enjoy him forever." There are no little places. Placement alone never makes us holy.

You glorify God by being a faithful member of your suburb. You glorify God when you ask God to open your eyes to the pain, hurt, and cracks beneath the pristine suburban surfaces of your own heart, home, and your next-door neighbor. You enjoy God when you live constantly in awe of his goodness to you, by a life marked by continual repentance, and as you learn to walk out of your belovedness. You glorify God when you practice hospitality, vulnerability, generosity, and strive for shalom in your subdivision. You glorify God when you stay put and stay small. God is a Father who runs to greet you, who goes out to meet you in your anger at the unfairness of life.

In the suburbs, we have bought the lie that our landscape proclaims: we are new and increasingly valuable, and we hide or distract ourselves from our brokenness. We put it behind pretty homes and well-behaved children. Finding holy in the suburbs starts with opening up the cracks that are already there—struggling marriages, fear about how our children will turn out, the financial stress of living beyond our means, a life with a full schedule but devoid of meaning. Your vulnerability and brokenness are a gift. They are not a liability.

Ann Voskamp writes her most recent book from the question, "How do you live with your own broken heart?" And how do you live in the suburbs when all around is slick surfaces and polite nods, but underneath you know that others—that you—are broken, falling apart, and insignificant? Do we keep pretending otherwise? Or can we open up the cracks of our humanity? That is, after all, how the light gets in. (Thanks, Leonard Cohen.) That's exactly how God gets in.

Wake up to your pain. Wake up to the pain of your neighbors. Only then are you awake to beauty, to flourishing, and to the God of glory, who can live anywhere, even in the suburbs. Modern-day Christians are often quick to pass over lament, the longing for shalom in our neighborhoods, suburbs, and cities, and tell ourselves a truncated version of glory.

The glory on the other side is so much richer. We quickly pass over brokenness, lament, and sin because we're desperate for a happy ending. We tell ourselves about being good, safe, and God's child, but we neglect to see how deep our own wells of brokenness are. When we cement over the cracks of sin in our hearts, lives, and neighborhoods, we cannot experience shalom in the suburbs. When we rush to the happy ending without moving through sin, repentance, and restoration, we sure can't experience foretastes of the glory of God. We cannot experience our longed-for unity around the marriage supper of the Lamb. We must stop tying up our stories in happy bows without first untying all the tangled roots of sin in our own hearts and the systems we're a part of.

We must own up to a view of suburban superiority that is not just *out there* but also *in here*. We must ask for the Spirit to plumb the depths of our hearts and follow the trails that show us we functionally trust our bank accounts, our education, our privilege, and our suburban bootstraps to save us. Like Martin Luther said, we can only get to a theology of glory through a theology of the cross.

The brokenness you embody, the pain your children experience, the hidden aches of your neighbors, and the impoverished among you are exactly the vehicle for knowing and loving Jesus. We can never get to glory without the cross.

GLORY AWAITS

We are placemakers. We long for a people and a place. We yearn for roots, while we also feel the pinch and urge to run away from all that threatens to hold us down. We turn our backs on the brokenness of the cross to try to pursue glory another way. It's the human way—to set off for the far country and try to make a name for ourselves, or to stay put and follow the rules thinking glory will come our way. If sin makes us homeless wanderers, it is right to weep for all we've lost, like God's people wept when their captors made them sing the songs of Zion (Psalm 137). We too must weep for our homeland that we've lost because of sin.

But the story doesn't stop in brokenhearted weeping. We are not stuck in an endless loop of shame. Just as our stories move toward redemption with the cross of Christ, our brokenheartedness moves toward a glorious homecoming.

The gospel is the glorious story of homecoming. God created place itself to have a *telos*; the places we inhabit are not dead-ends. We are going somewhere. Our suburbs, cities, the countryside, and small towns too are moving toward glory. We are all on the road home.

> Just as our stories move toward redemption with the cross of Christ, our brokenheartedness moves toward a glorious homecoming.

C. S. Lewis writes of our longing for home, our longing for glory, as finally being summoned in to the other side of the door that we've only seen from the outside. Our desire to fall into beauty, to "mingle with the pleasures we see," bubbles up in our shared human nostalgic ache for home. Lewis writes, "But all the leaves of the New Testament are rustling with the rumour that it will not always be so. Some day, God willing, we shall get *in*." The glory we chase in the suburbs—of faithful lovers, children, safety, comfort, leisure, freedom—will one day blossom not behind our picket fences but will spill out for all people and all places. What we term "successful" in the suburbs will be a pale comparison to the life-giving home of Glory himself.

For our coming glory is not a glory built on the backs of privilege, on the exploitation of racially "other" people. It is not a glory that is out for economic gain. It is glory that comes in blood and dirt and from a backwoods village. Ultimately, glory is Jesus himself. Like many asked when Jesus showed up, "Nazareth! Can anything good come from there?" (John 1:46), glory is not a state of being, a state of fame or success. *Glory* means "weighty," and the only one who can properly bear the weight of glory is Jesus.

But glory doesn't come how we think it should. That man from Galilee is the one who bears our suburban sins in his body and takes them to death. Three days later in a surprise that rolled like laughter at the very goodness and incredulity of it all, Jesus was raised from the dead. His resurrection shows us that all things—all hearts, all places—are being made new! That means you don't have to change the world—Jesus has already done that. That means you get to participate in the great story of glory that has come, is coming, and will come again.

You have nothing to prove by the size of your house, the success of your children, your safety, or your bank account and retirement plan. Because Jesus has borne all and been raised again, we can risk it all in lavish love. That means that you can stay put. That frees you to stay small. Invite someone to dinner, bring them to hear the gospel in your local church, give flowers to a neighbor, make margin in your schedule for God to show up and help you live a life committed to vulnerability, hospitality, generosity, and seeking the shalom of your suburb. God loves your suburb. It is good and right for you to love it well as you pour yourself out for it.

⌒☁☀☁⌒

I had supposed at the close of writing this book, I'd have a bag of glorious stories I could sprinkle like seed. I imagined I'd have found a home here. I'd be the intrepid guide to finding holy in the land of minivans, tract homes, and strip malls. I expected I'd begin the long, deep journey toward replanting myself in a place. Sure, I wouldn't have arrived, but I'd be well on my way: I'd be beginning to find my people; I'd be at home.

Instead, I have an even greater longing for home. Sometimes the way is hazy even as you commit, day by long day, to sink your roots into a place. Sometimes committing to a place and a people feels like eating vegetables because you know they are true nourishment, even when all you crave is salty potato chips and Swedish Fish. I still cry angry tears at God. I remember saying goodbye, running my fingers along the walls of our last house in Salt Lake City. Even as we paint walls here, preach a gospel of hospitality and vulnerability, and dream that the suburbs will be closer to glory, there is always that ache. And that's okay.

I have an itch to cut and run and drive my car as far as it will take me away from here. But there are peanut butter and jelly sandwiches to make. There are children to take to soccer. There are meals to bring to neighbors and a church I'm tethered to.

Belonging to a place means you rise and fall with it. It means you can't hover above it, bodiless, superior in thought, theology, and practice. Even still, "Strength comes, healing comes, from aligning yourself with the grain of your place and answering to its needs." For better or for worse, my place is this suburban spot of earth.

The only place of freedom I have to run to is Jesus, as I long for, look for, and work out the gospel in this suburb. I roll up my sleeves. I walk my suburban paths. When I crest the hill, I spread my hands like a prophet and ask God to rain down holy discontent and a hunger for him. I plead that he'd wake me—and these people—from my slumber, from the ways I numb pain with phones, exercise, sugar, or a glass of wine. From the ways that I reach back in time to find a perfect home "back then," or I dream about a future—using any memories to escape the here and now. We are homeless wanderers. On this side of glory, we will never be entirely at home. Like the desire to cut and run, the disappointment that God has not yet made all things new—including my at-home-ness in the suburbs—these aches point us homeward.

Maybe I wanted my pretty stories of finding holy in the suburbs more than the glory of Jesus. Glory always comes through the cross. It's part of your and my cross to live somewhere that will never entirely satisfy our hungers for home. Yet even though we ache, we choose to root ourselves on a ground that we might not find beautiful; we choose to remember our own particularities and culpabilities in the sins of our places; then, we will begin to long for glory.

Jesus is the glory we long for. He is the "radiance of the glory of God and the exact imprint of his nature, and he upholds the universe by the word of his power" (Hebrews 1:3). He is the light eternal. The Word before all time. Jesus alone is the glorious One. Only as I live out his story will I find holy in the suburbs. Glory is coming. Not yours. No, the glory that is coming is so much better than suburban safety, pretty Instagram feeds, and children who get a job better than we did. Jesus alone can bear the weight of glory without exploiting, withdrawing, or suffering.

And one day, in a move that shows us how dearly God loves our places, we won't be taken out of the world, from all the pain and tears. We won't be raptured up to sing in disembodied souls on puffy clouds. No. One day, Glory himself will come. John writes of the end:

> I saw the holy city, new Jerusalem, coming down out of heaven from God, prepared as a bride adorned for her husband. And I heard a loud voice from the throne saying, "Behold, the dwelling place of God is with man. He will dwell with them, and they will be his people, and God himself will be with them as their God. He will wipe away every tear from their eyes, and death shall be no more, neither shall there be mourning, nor crying, nor pain anymore, for the former things have passed away." (Revelation 21:2-4)

The Alpha and the Omega will say, "It is done!" echoing Jesus' "It is finished" on the cross. There is no more hustle. No more striving. No more ache. There is just the falling into beauty and glory itself. John

Home will come and get us.

is carried away in a vision to see "the Bride, the wife of the Lamb." He sees God's bride, the church, "the holy city Jerusalem coming down out of heaven from God, having the glory of God, its radiance like the most rare jewel" (Revelation 21:10-11). In your corner of the earth, in your tract home, your subdivision, your SUV or minivan, your picket fence, and your automatic garage door, you are radiant as you image Glory himself.

The story of the suburbs is still being written. One day, heaven will come out of the clouds—the new city—and that heaven on earth will be somehow better than Eden, for having been first lost, but redeemed, renewed, and regained. There, as in the words of the great hymn, glory will be God himself, "Our shelter from the stormy blast, / And our eternal home." Because God is our home, we can be home anywhere. As we find our home in God, Christ is formed in us, the hope of glory—even in the suburbs (Colossians 1:27).

Glory awaits and glory will come. And when glory comes, we will be home. Praise God! Home will come and get us.

PRACTICES

of Living into Glory

1. *Meditate on God's glory.* Read Isaiah 6, and consider God's glory and the response. Pray for eyes to see his glory in the everyday.

2. *Past, present, future prayers.* Focus your prayers on your future hope in heaven. Ask for forgiveness for your past sins, and ask that a future hope would ground your present love and work in your suburb.

3. *Immerse yourself in the Gospels.* For a season such as Advent or Lent, read the Gospels. Reflect on the glory of God in the incarnation, how Jesus was intimate and also glorious throughout his life, death, and resurrection, and ultimately how we receive the benefits of his glory through the Holy Spirit.

4. *Appreciate great art.* When our imaginations are captivated by beauty, we reach for transcendence, and it can turn us toward God. Practice awe and beauty as you make plans to visit an art gallery, see a play, listen to a musical performance, or read a classic book.

5. *Start a book club or service group.* Get people in your suburb to meet monthly to discuss the themes in this book (see pp. 175–76). Practice intentionally serving the needs of your community together. Create service challenges that work for your particular suburb.

ACKNOWLEDGMENTS

EVEN THOUGH MOST OF THE WORDS OF THIS BOOK were written while I sat on our old green couch before my family awoke, writing is never done in isolation. *Finding Holy in the Suburbs* only came to print because people believed not only in a first-time author, but also they believe we need words to help us find our way home—in the suburbs and around the world.

Thank you to Cindy Bunch and Anna Gissing, friends and editors, who helped me to kill my darlings. They helped me let go of some of my favorite parts of the book because they didn't serve the reader. I appreciate Helen Lee and our wonderful conversation at the Festival of Faith and Writing, which eventually led to this book. Thank you to the fabulous marketing team at IVP and all the small steps along the way that has made working with InterVarsity Press a joy.

This book would not be where it is without dear friends and fellow writers who pushed back, cheered me on, and those who'd gone ahead of me in this publishing journey. Thank you Emily Freeman for choosing to take a chance and write a gorgeous foreword to this book. I owe you a huge debt of gratitude for making time to read, comment, and tend to this book in your own busy season. It's no small thing to attach your name to a book. I love how even though each of us might be rooted in our own cul-de-sacs, together we can create cultures of hospitality, knowing we're connected in the mission of Jesus.

I owe a huge debt of gratitude to so many writers who cleared their schedule to read my book and write endorsements. The generosity of writers who have come before me and have in turn extended that generosity to me in endorsing this book helps encourage this calling.

Creating a writerly community has sustained the quiet hours of writing. A special thank you to Jen Pollock Michel for hours of Voxer conversations, for reading early drafts, generously endorsing the book, and connecting me with others. Abby Perry and Grace Cho were kind and helpful early readers; they are women worthy of entrusting my first draft to. Thank you to Aleah Marsden, Bronwyn Lea, Alia Joy, Shannan Martin, Cara Meredith, and Laura Fabrycky for keeping me sane via Voxer and writing retreats. The women at The Mudroom, Redbud Writers Guild, and The Well were a wealth of encouragement, joy, and support in the process. I'm so grateful to be a part of these writing communities.

Thank you to my fellow pastors' wives, the "city wives" of Salt Lake City, who initially nurtured and held my writing. To Kate Wheatley, Stephanie McKinney, Amy Warmath, and Melissa Peach for the beauty of eating breakfast together and praying for years. Though we're spread from New York City to California now, in cities and suburbs, thank you for those sweet years of loving Jesus together. Thank you to Mark and Melissa Peach for being those friends we can always run to.

The largest debts of book writing are always closest to home. A huge thank you to my parents, Tor and Carolyn Hutchins, for watching my kids and always being my biggest cheerleaders for almost four decades. Thank you to my in-laws, John and Sally Hales, who generously offer support, babysitting, and a glass of wine. A particular thank you to Carter and Kerry Crockett, who have modeled loving their people and place well, wherever God has called them.

The people of Resurrection OC, our church plant in the Southern California suburbs, have been amazing. They have loved me, prayed for me, and regularly asked how the book was coming along. They also surrounded me with prayer and practical help: thank you to Nancy,

Renon, Trudy, Karla, Alita, Ashlee, and others for praying, encouraging, and watching my children so I could write. The people of ResOC love Jesus and know how to throw a good party. I am blessed to find holy in the suburbs alongside you.

My children mistakenly think they have a famous mom now that I'll have a book on the shelves. While fame is never the goal, I could not have explored this writing journey without their constant kindness. Thank you to Ezra, Porter, Camden, and Harriet for family dance parties, for letting their mom run away to write, and for heaps of grace, forgiveness, and love in the process. It is my prayer that God will always run after you, that you'll learn to love the places God will direct you to, and that you always know you have a place to come home to no matter what.

Thank you to my husband, Bryce. You have become increasingly dear to me through the writing of this book. That you pastor your people so well, giving invisibly and vulnerably of yourself, inspires me daily. I've seen God work so much grace in you through our move to the suburbs. I'll live in the suburbs for the rest of my life if you do it with me. You are mine, always.

Thank you to my Lord and Savior, Jesus Christ, who gave up his life so I could be close to him. God, you've shown yourself to be the Father who runs to meet us at the end of the road and goes out to meet us in our stubborn pride. Thank you for writing my story, for leading me from a home I loved into the suburbs, a place I'm learning to love. Jesus, thank you for being the prize no matter where we live.

Finally, thank you, my reader. Thank you for your time, attention, and kindness in your willingness to be transformed by words. Thank you to those who've helped me process the message of Finding Holy in the Suburbs through speaking engagements. It's been my pleasure to sharpen one another as we seek to live out gospel hospitality. And now, dear reader, may the smile of the Father rest on you and make you glad as you seek to find holy in the suburbs.

DISCUSSION
QUESTIONS

1. In the introduction, Ashley writes about being unsettled after her move home to the suburbs. What is your attitude about where you live? About the suburbs? Are you content, unsettled, unaware of how your environment affects you, or something else?

2. Ashley writes, "Feeling our hunger is the first step to remembering who we are." What are you hungry for? Consider together: What does your particular suburb or neighborhood hunger for? How does Jesus meet these hungers?

3. Where have you followed your hungers to buy (consumerism) or to center yourself (individualism)? What practical habits can you take as a group to grow generosity?

4. Throughout the book and especially in chapter three, Ashley mentions time as a commodity. We either give it or take it. How can you use your time as an individual, family, or church community for the good of others?

5. Think together about safety and what your attitudes are toward it. Where does it fit on your list of life goals ("If I have X, I'll be okay")? Is there a way to make wider circles of belonging in your neighborhood? What might that look like for your group?

6. In chapter six, Ashley writes, "Love does not leave us where it finds us." What blinders about your own suburban way of life do you need to take off? Where do you need to repent or forgive others so you can live out the welcome of Jesus in your neighborhood and church?

7. In chapter seven, how does the cross model hospitality for you? How does this free you up to offer yourself vulnerably for your suburb? Spend some time brainstorming together what this could look like on the ground.

8. In chapter nine, Ashley writes about being birthed into vulnerability where we can embrace meaningful risk. What risks have you taken that might look boring and ordinary? What risks can you take as a group?

9. In chapter ten on shalom, Ashley writes, "Your dreams of the good life will have to be swallowed up into the sweeter story of the gospel, whose narrative arc never has us at its center, but God alone." What about this scares you? Excites you?

10. In the conclusion, Ashley writes about a dinner where she experienced what felt like an appetizer of God's kingdom. Have you had moments where your life has been reframed, or where you've tangibly experienced God's goodness? How might experiencing these moments, chronicling them, and looking for them help you love your suburb more day to day?

11. Which chapter got under your skin or stuck with you the most? Where do you sense a kind invitation to repent? Or where are you motivated to work toward change in your suburb?

12. Ashley writes, "Belonging to a place means you rise and fall with it." What does belonging to your place look like for you as an individual, family, or group? Dream together about what groups and churches seeking to find holy in the suburbs could do.

13. What was the most surprising thing to you about this book?

14. What action step will you take now to find holy in your suburb?

NOTES

INTRODUCTION

8   *Are the suburbs really the "geography of nowhere"*: James Howard Kunstler, *The Geography of Nowhere* (New York: Simon & Schuster, 1993).

9   *the suburbs "built inequality to last"*: Becky M. Nicolaides and Andrew Wiese, eds., *The Suburb Reader* (New York: Routledge, 2006), 6.

14 *God needs suburban Christians*: Albert Y. Hsu, *The Suburban Christian: Finding Spiritual Vitality in the Land of Plenty* (Downers Grove, IL: InterVarsity Press, 2006), 183.

1 WORSHIPING GRANITE COUNTERTOPS

21 *Definition of salvation*: "Salvation," *OED Online*, accessed June 2017, www.oed.com/viewdictionaryentry/Entry/11125.

   God's people are not freed: John L. Mackay, *Exodus* (Fearn, UK: Mentor, 2001), 10.

22 *consumerism is a type of spirituality*: William T. Cavanaugh, *Being Consumed: Economics and Christian Desire* (Grand Rapids: Eerdmans, 2008), 44.

23 *There is an intimate and indissoluble link*: Roger Silverstone, ed., *Visions of Suburbia* (New York: Rutledge, 1997), 8.

   we come looking: James K. A. Smith, *Desiring the Kingdom: Worship, Worldview, and Cultural Formation* (Grand Rapids: Baker, 2009), 22.

   newfound holy object in hand: Ibid.

25 *What if "my daily practices [are] malforming me"*: Tish Harrison Warren, *Liturgy of the Ordinary: Sacred Practices in Everyday Life* (Downers Grove, IL: InterVarsity Press, 2016), 31.

26 *You see, we were passionate then*: Carol Ann Duffy, "Mrs. Midas," in *Poetry 180: A Turning Back to Poetry*, ed. Billy Collins (New York: Random House, 2003), 51.

   I miss most: Ibid., 52.

26   *It is not objects that people really desire*: Neil Cummings and Marysia Lewandowska, quoted in James B. Twitchell, *Branded Nation: The Marketing
of Megachurch, College Inc., and Museumworld* (New York: Simon &
Schuster, 2004), 37.

29   *of course we are meant to eat*: Andy Crouch, *The Tech-Wise Family:
Everyday Steps for Putting Technology in Its Proper Place* (Grand Rapids:
Baker, 2017), 37.

     Things are not ends in themselves: Cavanaugh, *Being Consumed*, 58.

30   *every square inch*: Abraham Kuyper, quoted in James D. Bratt, ed., *Abraham
Kuyper: A Centennial Reader* (Grand Rapids: Eerdmans, 1998), 488.

     They are only the scent of a flower: C. S. Lewis, *The Weight of Glory* (New
York: HarperCollins, 1949), 31.

2 WHEN YOUR WORTH IS MEASURED
IN SQUARE FOOTAGE

34   *There is no object of desire*: Meghan Daum, *Life Would Be Perfect If I Lived
in That House* (New York: Alfred A. Knopf, 2010), 4, 5.

     America's national housing policy: Matthew Desmond, "How Homeown-
ership Became the Engine of American Inequality," *New York Times Magazine*, May 9, 2017, https://nyti.ms/2pZp92k.

35   *Hispanic Americans are 78 percent*: Gillian B. White, "Why Blacks and His-
panics Have Such Expensive Mortgages," *Atlantic*, February 25, 2016, www
.theatlantic.com/business/archive/2016/02/blacks-hispanics-mortgages
/471024.

     eminently chaseable: Meghan Daum, "What Makes a House a Home?," *Literary
Hub*, May 10, 2017, http://lithub.com/what-makes-a-house-a-home.

     sovereign chooser: William T. Cavanaugh, *Being Consumed: Economics and
Christian Desire* (Grand Rapids: Eerdmans, 2008), 53.

36   *The individual, unlike the household*: Wendell Berry, "Sex, Economy,
Freedom, and Community," *Sex, Economy, Freedom & Community: Eight
Essays* (New York: Pantheon, 1992), 149.

37   *escape from the constraints of community*: Berry, "Sex, Economy, Freedom,
and Community," 149.

     If your story of redemption stops: Mike Wilkerson, *Redemption: Freed by
Jesus from the Idols We Worship and the Wounds We Carry* (Wheaton, IL:
Crossway, 2011), 172.

38   *God "wants to do something in you"*: Ibid.

      aligning [ourselves] with the grain of [our] place: Scott Russell Sanders, *Staying Put: Making Home in a Restless World* (Boston: Beacon Press, 1993), 120.

40   *It's such an odd sort of mercy*: Graham Greene, *The End of the Affair* (New York: Penguin, 1951), 146.

43   *We are given a double portion*: This section comes from Bryce Hales's sermon "Comfort," Resurrection Orange County, December 19, 2016, https://resoc.podbean.com/e/comfort-1505863844.

      relatively unconditional life of the public: Berry, "Sex, Economy, Freedom, and Community," 149.

44   *moved by the signs of what it cost to bring [us] home*: Timothy Keller, *The Prodigal God* (New York: Dutton, 2008), 86.

      I had tried to be happy: G. K. Chesterton, *Orthodoxy* (New York and London: John Lane, 1908), 147.

45   *rock that does not move*: Sandra McCracken, "Steadfast," *God's Highway,* Drink Your Tea Music, 2016.

3 CIRCLING THE SUBURBS IN MY MINIVAN

49   *the shift from leisure-as-status*: Silvia Bellezza, Neeru Pahari, and Anat Keinan, "Research: Why Americans Are So Impressed by Busyness," *Harvard Business Review,* December 15, 2016, https://hbr.org/2016/12/research-why-americans-are-so-impressed-by-busyness.

      essential element of identity: Joe Pinsker, "'Ugh, I'm So Busy': A Status Symbol for Our Time," *Atlantic*, March 1, 2017, www.theatlantic.com/business/archive/2017/03/busyness-status-symbol/518178.

51   *equivalent of seven forty-hour work weeks*: AAA Foundation for Traffic Safety, accessed September 3, 2017, www.aaafoundation.org/sites/default/files/2015AmericanDrivingSurveyFS.pdf.

51   *People began to learn*: Judith Shulevitz, *The Sabbath World: Glimpses of a Different Order of Time* (New York: Random House, 2010), 96.

54   *All these giants of the faith*: Marlena Graves, *A Beautiful Disaster: Finding Hope in the Midst of Brokenness* (Grand Rapids: Brazos, 2014), 6-7.

55   *God set up a yearly holiday*: Nancy Guthrie, *One Year of Dinner Table Devotions and Discussion Starters* (Carol Stream, IL: Tyndale House, 2008), 262.

57   *Part of living well in ordinary time*: Emily P. Freeman, *Simply Tuesday: Small-Moment Living in a Fast-Paced World* (Grand Rapids: Revell, 2015), 235.

4 BEYOND THE GATED COMMUNITY

61   *offered what suburban developers*: Edward J. Blakely and Mary Gail Snyder, *Fortress America: Gated Communities in the United States* (Washington, DC: Brookings Institution Press, 1995), ebook.

62   *The problem with gated communities*: Andres Duany, Elizabeth Plater-Zyberk, and Jeff Speck, *Suburban Nation: The Rise of Sprawl and the Decline of the American Dream* (New York: North Point Press, 2010), 45.

65   *controlling and overinvolved parents*: Madeline Levine, *The Price of Privilege: How Parental Pressure and Material Advance Are Creating a Generation of Disconnected and Unhappy Kids* (New York: Harper, 2008), 31.

      emotional and psychological problems: Ibid., 21.

68   *sometimes surrender means letting go*: Shannan Martin, *Falling Free: Rescued from the Life I Always Wanted* (Nashville: Thomas Nelson, 2016), 110.

69   *"hyphenated" sins of the human spirit*: A. W. Tozer, *The Pursuit of God* (Bromley, UK: STL Books, 1984), 45.

5 WHERE THE SIDEWALK ENDS

72   *interview with Frank Wilczek*: Frank Wilczek, "Why Is the World So Beautiful?," *On Being*, April 28, 2016, www.onbeing.org/program/frank-wilczek-why-is-the-world-so-beautiful/transcript/8632.

73   *grasped by what we cannot grasp*: Rainer Marie Rilke, "A Walk," https://allpoetry.com/a-walk.

81   *always and everywhere the first word*: Eugene H. Peterson, *A Long Obedience in the Same Direction: Discipleship in an Instant Society*, 2nd ed. (Downers Grove, IL: InterVarsity Press, 2000), 29.

      a rejection that is also an acceptance: Ibid., 33.

      get fed up with the ways of the world: Ibid., 25.

82   *repentance always ends in rejoicing*: The stages of repentance are helpfully articulated in Mike Wilkerson, *Redemption: Freed by Jesus from the Idols We Worship and the Wounds We Carry* (Wheaton, IL: Crossway, 2011).

      what we have done: "A Penitential Order: Rite One," *The (Online) Book of Common Prayer*, accessed January 8, 2017, www.bcponline.org/HE/penord1.html.

84 *God's reckless grace*: Timothy Keller, *The Prodigal God* (New York: Dutton, 2008), xx.

generous release of a genuine debt: Miroslav Volf, *Free of Charge: Giving and Forgiving in a Culture Stripped of Grace* (Grand Rapids: Zondervan, 2005), 130.

we fall on the grenade: I'm indebted to Rev. Sam Wheatley, our pastor at New Song Presbyterian (Salt Lake City) and now at Redeemer Presbyterian Church (New York City) for this image.

6 YOU'RE NOT A BARBIE, YOU BELONG

93 *The whole of God's story*: Mike Wilkerson, *Redemption: Freed by Jesus from the Idols We Worship and the Wounds We Carry* (Wheaton, IL: Crossway, 2011), 158.

94 *Jesus is eternally beloved*: Tish Harrison Warren, *Liturgy of the Ordinary: Sacred Practices in Everyday Life* (Downers Grove, IL: InterVarsity Press, 2016), 17.

96 *cheap grace*: This phrase comes from Dietrich Bonhoeffer's *The Cost of Discipleship* (New York: Touchstone, 1995), 43.

People are limited: Henri Nouwen, "Solitude, Community, and Ministry: Three Ways to Create Space for God," *30 Good Minutes*, November 7, 1993, www.30goodminutes.org/index.php/archives/23-member-archives/352 -henri-nouwen-program-3706.

97 *surrounds us like a house*: Luci Shaw, *Breath for the Bones: Art, Imagination, and Spirit* (Nashville: Thomas Nelson, 2009), xii.

the infinite abyss: Blaise Pascal, *Pensées,* 7.425, trans. F. W. Trotter, www .ccel.org/ccel/pascal/pensees.viii.html.

the only way to dispossess: Thomas Chalmers, "The Expulsive Power of a New Affection," Christianity.com, accessed February 2, 2017, www .christianity.com/christian-life/spiritual-growth/the-expulsive-power-of -a-new-affection-11627257.html.

98 *Thou didst call and cry aloud*: Augustine, *Confessions*, bk. 10, chap. 27. www.sacred-texts.com/chr/augconf/aug10.htm.

happy island: Chalmers, "The Expulsive Power of a New Affection."

99 *signals of welcome*: Chalmers, "The Expulsive Power of a New Affection."

He is good, but he is not tame: In C. S. Lewis's *The Lion, The Witch and the Wardrobe*, when Susan asks if the lion Aslan is safe, Mr. Beaver says,

"Course he isn't safe. But he's good." C. S. Lewis, *The Lion, The Witch and the Wardrobe* (New York: HarperCollins, 1998), 81.

100   *He is our guide and horizon*: Rankin Wilbourne, *Union with Christ: The Way to Know and Enjoy God* (Colorado Springs: David C. Cook, 2016), 217.

7 THIS ISN'T PINTEREST-WORTHY ENTERTAINING

106   *fleshly actuality*: Fleming Rutledge, *The Crucifixion: Understanding the Death of Jesus Christ* (Grand Rapids: Eerdmans, 2017), 79.

109   *they were talking about something bigger*: N. T. Wright, *The Day the Revolution Began: Reconsidering the Meaning of Jesus's Crucifixion* (San Francisco: HarperOne, 2016), 4.

       As Christians became more established: Christine D. Pohl, *Making Room: Recovering Hospitality as a Christian Tradition* (Grand Rapids: Eerdmans, 1999), 113.

111   *the crisis in hospitality*: Sarah Arthur and Erin F. Wasinger, *The Year of Small Things* (Grand Rapids: Brazos Press, 2017), 42.

       what is countercultural in the United States: Gerald W. Schlabach, "The Virtue of Staying Put: What the 'Benedict Option' Forgets About Benedictines," *Commonweal*, September 26, 2016, www.commonwealmagazine .org/virtue-staying-put.

8 OPEN HEARTS AND OPEN HANDS

118   *The rich are not necessarily wicked*: Craig L. Blomberg, *Neither Poverty Nor Riches: A Biblical Theology of Possessions* (Downers Grove, IL: InterVarsity Press, 1999), 246.

       It seems that insulation from people: Ken Stern, "Why the Rich Don't Give to Charity," *Atlantic*, April 2013, www.theatlantic.com/magazine /archive/2013/04/why-the-rich-dont-give/309254.

119   *generosity does not affect our actual day-to-day lives*: Tim Keller, *Generous Justice: How God's Grace Makes Us Just* (New York: Penguin, 2008), 113.

       It is not uncommon for people to think: Dallas Willard, *The Divine Conspiracy: Recovering Our Hidden Life in God* (San Francisco: HarperCollins, 1998), 207.

125   *If God's character includes a zeal*: Keller, *Generous Justice*, 8.

9 THE OPPORTUNITY OF CUL-DE-SACS

131 *vulnerability is the birthplace of creativity*: Brené Brown, "Brené Brown at TED2012," *TEDBlog*, March 2, 2012, http://blog.ted.com/vulnerability-is -the-birthplace-of-innovation-creativity-and-change-brene-brown-at -ted2012.

132 *exposure to meaningful risk*: Andy Crouch, *Strong and Weak: Embracing a Life of Love, Risk and True Flourishing* (Downers Grove, IL: InterVarsity Press, 2016), 40.

133 *we can't selectively numb emotion*: Brené Brown, *Daring Greatly: How the Courage to Be Vulnerable Transforms the Way We Live, Love, Parent and Lead* (New York: Penguin, 2012), 138.

a wounded healer who has gone before us: This is Henri Nouwen's phrase from his book *The Wounded Healer* (New York: Doubleday, 1972).

135 *hyphenated sins of the human spirit*: A. W. Tozer, *The Pursuit of God* (Bromley, UK: STL Books, 1984), 45.

137 *the surrendering of a space*: Hak Joon Lee, "Kingdom and Kenosis: The Mind of Christ in Paul's Ethics," *FullerStudio*, accessed March 17, 2017, https://fullerstudio.fuller.edu/kingdom-and-kenosis-the-mind-of-christ -in-pauls-ethics. Originally published as "Have This Mind Among You: Philippians 2:1-11," *Theology, News & Notes*, Fall 2013.

137 *Paul is directly telling*: Lee, "Kingdom and Kenosis."

Build cul-de-sacs where neighbors: Thomas R. Hochschild Jr., quoted in Emily Badger, "The Case for Cul-de-Sacs," *CityLab*, October 17, 2013, www.citylab.com/housing/2013/10/sociologists-defense-cul-de-sac/7262.

139 *Church is not meant to be*: Matthew S. Farlow, "In Pursuit of a Consumer Crown or a Crucified Crown?," in *Theology and California: Theological Reflections on California's Culture*, ed. Fred Sanders and Jason S. Sexton (Surrey, UK: Ashgate, 2014), 123.

10 PAPER BIRDS AND HUMAN FLOURISHING

144 *Home represents humanity's most visceral ache*: Jen Pollock Michel, *Keeping Place: Reflections on the Meaning of Home* (Downers Grove, IL: Inter- Varsity Press, 2017), 28.

146 *At the core of biblical narrative*: Kelton Cobb, "Fourth Sunday of Lent," in *Feasting on the Word: A Thematic Resource for Preaching and Worship, Lenten Companion*, ed. David L. Bartlett, Barbara Brown Taylor, and Kim- berly Bracken Long (Louisville, KY: Westminster John Knox, 2014), 84.

147   *The webbing together of God*: Cornelius Plantinga Jr., *Not the Way It's Supposed to Be: A Breviary of Sin* (Grand Rapids: Eerdmans, 1995), 10.

156   *faithful presence within*: James Davison Hunter, *To Change the World: The Irony, Tragedy, and Possibility of Christianity in the Late Modern World* (Oxford: Oxford University Press, 2010), 277.

      As they pursued: Hunter, *To Change the World*, 277.

157   *surrender to it, and suffer with it*: Kathleen Norris, *The Cloister Walk* (New York: Riverhead, 1997), 244.

158   *When we begin to dream about our cities*: Sarah Arthur and Erin F. Wasinger, *The Year of Small Things: Radical Faith for the Rest of Us* (Grand Rapids: Brazos Press, 2017), 195.

      Let us run, skip, jump, twirl, and dance: Osheta Moore, *Shalom Sistas: Living Wholeheartedly in a Brokenhearted World* (Harrisonburg, VA: Herald Press, 2017), 221.

159   *more devoted to "order" than to justice*: Martin Luther King Jr., "Letter from a Birmingham Jail," University of Pennsylvania, April 16, 1963, www.africa.upenn.edu/Articles_Gen/Letter_Birmingham.html.

CONCLUSION

164   *to glorify God, and to enjoy him forever*: Westminster Shorter Catechism, question 1, www.reformed.org/documents/wsc/index.html.

165   *How do you live with your own broken heart?*: Ann Voskamp, *The Broken Way: A Daring Path to the Abundant Life* (Grand Rapids: Zondervan, 2017).

167   *We are going somewhere*: Leonard Hjalmarson, *No Home Like Place: A Christian Theology of Place* (Portland, OR: Urban Loft, 2015), 75.

      But all the leaves of the New Testament: C. S. Lewis, *The Weight of Glory* (New York: HarperCollins, 1949), 43.

169   *Strength comes, healing comes*: Scott Russell Sanders, *Staying Put: Making a Home in a Restless World* (Boston: Beacon Press, 1993), 120.

171   *Our shelter from the stormy blast*: Isaac Watts, "Our God, Our Help in Ages Past," Church of God Music, accessed January 10, 2018, www.cgmusic.org/workshop/watts/wpsalm90.htm.